COLD DEEP WATERS

An Autobiography

The Mystery, Secret and Revelation
The Hidden and Forgotten Royal Line

L. J. Hobson

Disclaimer

This is my grandmother's story. It is a true account that records conversations and information passed to me in early 1960. To the best of my knowledge, memory and recollection, the following story and information is factual.

Published in Australia by Sid Harta Publishers Pty Ltd,
ABN: 46 119 415 842
23 Stirling Crescent, Glen Waverley, Victoria 3150 Australia
Telephone: +61 3 9560 9920, Facsimile: +61 3 9545 1742
E-mail: author@sidharta.com.au

First published in Australia 2019
This edition published 2019
Copyright © L.J. Hobson 2019
Cover design, typesetting: WorkingType (www.workingtype.com.au)

The right of L.J. Hobson to be identified as the Author of the Work has been asserted in accordance with the Copyright, Designs and Patents Act 1988.

This book is a work of fiction. Any similarities to that of people living or dead are purely coincidental.

The Author of this book accepts all responsibility for the contents and absolves any other person or persons involved in its production from any responsibility or liability where the contents are concerned.

All rights reserved. No part of this publication may be reproduced, stored in a retrieval system, or transmitted, in any form or by any means without the prior written permission of the publisher, nor be otherwise circulated in any form of binding or cover other than that in which it is published and without a similar condition being imposed on the subsequent purchaser.

L.J. Hobson
Cold Deep Waters: An Autobiography. The Mystery, Secret and Revelation of the Hidden and Forgotten Royal Line
ISBN: 978-0-6484916-0-6
pp158

A Tribute

Wonderful memories of my beautiful and dear mother, June. I will forever love and miss your smile, chuckle and zest for life. You passed way too early in 2006. Forever in our hearts.

My Family

You are my rock. You never leave me. You are simply the best and mean everything in life to me. Thank goodness the family has grown significantly and brought with it so much love happiness and laughter.

About the Author

What pleasure and enjoyment I have shared in raising three children and recently welcoming our first wonderful granddaughter into the family!

The author would like to be known as a positive, happy, no fuss, practical and independent person.

Combined interests operating as an interior decorator over the last 35 years including contracts with the major paint companies. Eight years in a specialist federal government agency. Now seemingly turned author!

Thank You

The Kershaw family. What a marvellous family you are. You were always there to lend a helping hand. True friendship is hard to find. Your kindness never forgotten.

To my dear friends Lily and Greg Bond for a lifetime of friendship.

Lily you are the most beautiful woman I have known and the most strong and resilient. You were one of the many female trailblazers to hold office on the board of directors of the very old and popular Bronte R.S.L. Club in Sydney. What a woman.

Greg, we were school chums. We grew up together as teenagers swimming many hours in the beautiful ocean of our most loved La Perouse where you dedicated most of your adult life as a land conservationist and environmentalist. You have been a great advocate for people's rights, and importantly you were such a valiant crusader for my family.

Thank you to Daphne Douglas McKenna and Ray McKenna — you are the salt of the earth and tar for being instrumental in referring me to my publishers. Divine intervention; the same namesake as my Aunty Daphne Douglass in this book.

Dear and caring Lorraine. To you and your delightful family. Thank you for your true kindness. We have many similarities in life.

Contents

Preface	1
Dedication	7
Castle Life is Short Lived	19
The Hobson Line	33
Lady Ursula	61
Secrets, Castle Conversations and Deja vu	73
Life in an Idyllic Coastal Village	77
Troubled Waters Again – Farewell William Farrell	104
The Shark Arm Murder Mystery	112
The Royal Truth Finally Uncovered	116
Epilogue	126

The Hidden and Forgotten Royal Line of Q. Victoria and John Brown

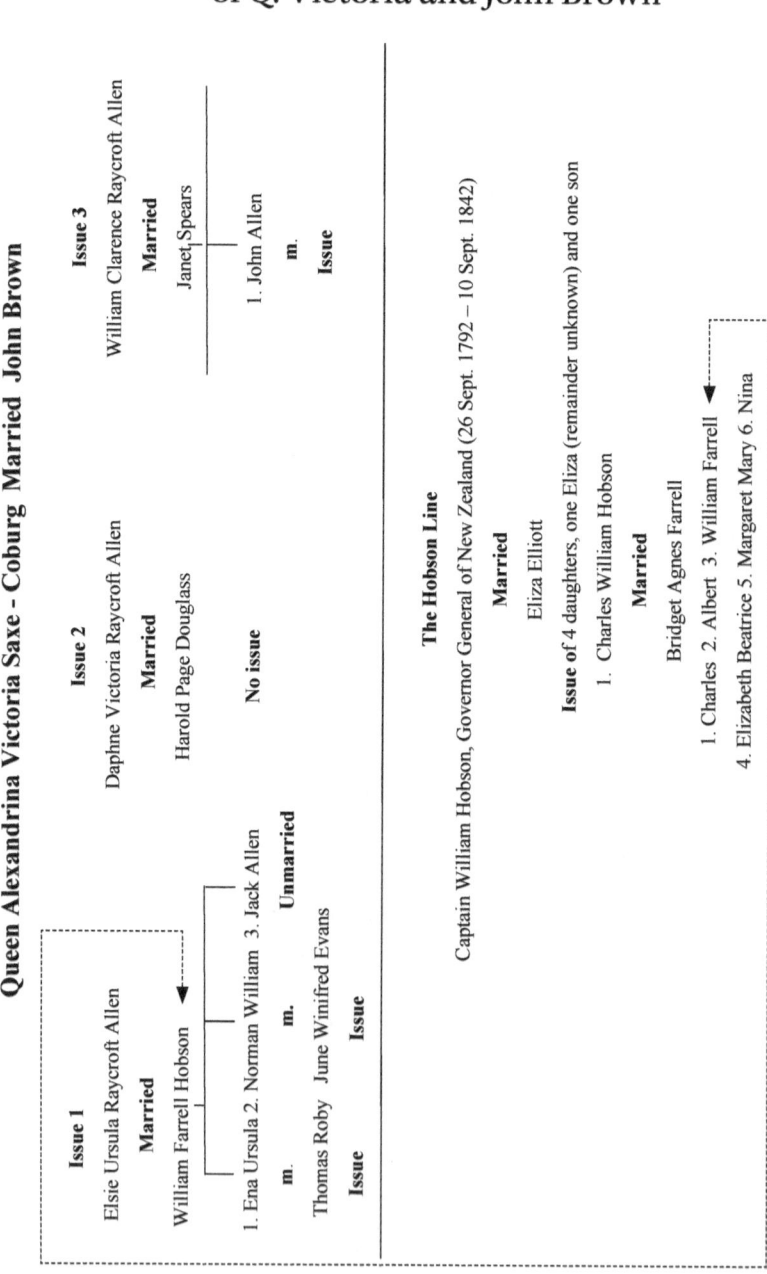

Queen Alexandrina Victoria Saxe - Coburg Married John Brown

Issue 1	Issue 2	Issue 3
Elsie Ursula Raycroft Allen	Daphne Victoria Raycroft Allen	William Clarence Raycroft Allen
Married	Married	Married
William Farrell Hobson	Harold Page Douglass	Janet Spears
1. Ena Ursula 2. Norman William 3. Jack Allen	No issue	1. John Allen
m. Unmarried		m.
Thomas Roby June Winifred Evans		Issue
Issue Issue		

The Hobson Line

Captain William Hobson, Governor General of New Zealand (26 Sept. 1792 – 10 Sept. 1842)

Married

Eliza Elliott

Issue of 4 daughters, one Eliza (remainder unknown) and one son

1. Charles William Hobson

Married

Bridget Agnes Farrell

1. Charles 2. Albert 3. William Farrell
4. Elizabeth Beatrice 5. Margaret Mary 6. Nina

NB. Please note that this family tree is accurate from information passed and sources available to me at the time of print.
Cold Deep Waters Autobiography July 2019

Preface

The mystery surrounding Queen Victoria and John Brown and the heightened rumours of an offspring has always been a hot topic, and one which has been bandied throughout the corridors of history. The story was nonetheless enthralling for me, due mainly to the fact that I had been privy to some of the royal inner secrets which had been passed to me by my grandmother Elsie Ursula. As a child it was mere information and although I had been engrossed in the detail, I sadly took for granted the importance of her messages.

There has been little consultation with any other party on the information contained in this book. It is the factual account of my family's journey, lineage and legacy however extraordinary. You be the judge.

After my grandmother's passing in 1982, I was to question my knowledge and memory from 'those talks' on the topic of 'royal matters.' I was also confused why my grandmother and her two siblings, Daphne and William arrived in Australia under a cloak of secrecy from England in a private voyage accompanied by Victoria's entrusted lady-in-waiting, Annie and a Security Minder. Had they done something so wrong that they were banished to a remote country?

My investigation began and I found it astonishing why any progeny of Victoria and John had vanished without a trace in the world. My mind raced as possibility that my grandmother could be THAT lost child…but knowing also the rumour that one child had been born to Queen Victoria and John Brown, how did it fit that my grandmother Elsie Ursula journeyed from England with a sister and a brother?

Was it possible that Victoria had given birth to three children by John Brown and not one? During my research, I discovered an article which alluded to there being a concealed royal offspring from that union.

There was further information on historical

websites also alluding to there being three children born to Victoria and John.

Based upon these facts and my discussions with grandmother Ursula, I am brazenly asserting that she WAS the first of three children born to Victoria and John Brown. My grandmother's birthday was always celebrated on 24 May which was Victoria's birthday! Although gran's real birth date is 23 May. This must be one of the better kept secrets of the world.

In my wildest dreams I did not realise that I would be the key or source to the royal mystery. Thank you grandmother for your trust and wisdom in choosing me as your messenger. Grandmother spoke of 'her mother' without ever uttering her name. I gather from this that they had sworn or taken a pledge not to disclose the secret pact and moreover not to endanger their families. Although remarks did disclose that her father suffered with a rash on his face called erysipelas and he had once caught pneumonia whilst walking in the rain.

It is now obvious as I oversee our family photographs. The likeness between our families is significant. Therefore, the Saxe-Coburg Gotha noses are certainly a prominent feature, and grandmother Ursula is almost a twin for Princess Alice, Countess of Althone 1883-1981. My gran and I share similarities to Princess Marie. Ursula and her brother William are very similar facially but I have been unable to locate any photographs of her youngest sister Daphne for comparison. According to my father, Daphne was the closest in features and figure to Queen Victoria.

As I had detected as a very young girl my uncle Jack also resembles Prince Phillip Mountbatten and seems to share the same characteristics; particularly a witty sense of humour.

I have read previously that Victoria gave birth in or near Switzerland, therefore the name Ursula would resonate with that suggestion.

Understandably, there remains precious little documentation associated with events which occurred such a long time ago, but it would certainly be selfish not to share our memoirs and history with you all.

Is this whole story a revelation or a tragedy? How did our lives take such an acute turn? How was this executed and manoeuvred? For security purpose, the key players would have been minimal indeed. It is a revelation to also discover that our roots are in

England and we are really a displaced family! Prior to my grandmother, there appeared no family predecessors. No strata to her family. Where were our relatives? Certainly our relatives were not looking for us. They were not even in the same country. It may even explain why I always cry watching the Military Tattoo.

Sadness surrounds these matters. Were we not wanted? A cover up? Can I justify anger in what I do not fully understand? Is there more to come?

Was this secret ultimately meant to be discovered? Was there an error…was it for a short term only before everything went 'haywire'? Was there an unexpected intervention preventing a return of the family to their rightful place? The passage of time and contrived efforts may have forever swept away key traces during those early colonial days when passports were non-existent and lack of identification could make for successful unnoticed clandestine voyages.

To my grandmother and her two siblings, Daphne and William, this book serves as a tribute from your family and will perpetuate your memory.

Loving thoughts to William (Hobson), Ursula's husband and my grandfather. I have clarity in you being the chosen one to provide a name change through marriage which forever masked her royal connection. It has concerned me that you may have had no choice in royal matters.

From a royal perspective, the best way to secret the royal threads was to intertwine both women in society and marriage offered new surnames to legitimise and ensure their safety. Prior to those marriages and their arrival into Australia, Victoria's family of three were given to use the surname Alen (Allen).

Thank you for sharing their journey. It is and has been a monumental and heart-wrenching experience for me. Will you find it enthralling and provocative? I hope so!

You will also share family adventures on the high seas and an insight into Ursula's oh so ordinary life.

Dedication

This autobiography was never going to be an easy write. Particularly at the close, it has raised more questions than answers for me. What catastrophic events thrusted a family, carers and security minder to travel thousands of sailing miles in putrid conditions leaving behind the history and finery of England for a shattered and protracted life in a foreign and estranged country?

There has been much written on the reign of Her Royal Highness Alexandrina Victoria Saxe-Coburg Gotha and her family. There has been scant information but much innuendo surrounding the private and personal Victoria.

As I now realise, it is the dedication and allegiance

of Victoria's close confidants and personal assistants who were sworn to keep that privacy and those secrets.

The connection and love between a young girl and her elderly grandmother melted away a century and a half of secrets. My grandmother opened her heart and entrusted me with some startling revelations.

During my research in the late 1990's, I was to have a poignant telephone conversation with my cousin John Allen, Ursula's nephew and son of her brother William Allen. John had a keen interest in the military and was an active member of the Black Watch combined with an even keener interest in our family heritage.

By phone, we spoke at length of our concerns, research and findings. John was now confused that there was conflicting information surrounding grandmother's christian name, having always been called Elsie but now Ursula appears on her Marriage Certificate in 1912. The (mock) certificate identifies John Allen as her father's name but she only ever spoke about him as being Elias. On that basis, he pledged his research by email which arrived promptly. The email also consisted of a copy of inscriptions within the front cover of a small Bible.

Dedication

John remarked that the information was beginning to read like a Georgette Heyer novel. He impressed me to remain dedicated in tracing and solving our family heritage.

John sadly passed away in November 2009, but I am hopeful that he would be at peace with the resultant pages. For many years, my parents June and Norman William Hobson and my three faithful and dedicated followers, my children, have been included in the slow unravelling of this fascinating story.

As I move through these paragraphs it brings mixed emotions and lament. This story may even be remembered as one of the great love stories. It may validate Victoria's unswerving devotion and dedication to her role as Queen of England and to the Crown?

Perhaps we will question the see-sawing decisions she was required to make as a duteous mother to Albert's children as opposed to her family with John Brown.

Was Victoria really as autonomous and powerful upon the throne of England in matters of the heart, or were there certain pressures to bear from other quarters where it impacted negatively upon the royal house?

What prompted Queen Victoria to rear three young children with John within the palace grounds and then to have a change of heart, leaving no trace of the children's existence or their protectors. From my understanding, there were many royal homes upon the royal estates such as Balmoral or the Isle of Wight and further afield where three youngsters could have remained remote, home-schooled and completely self-sufficient and away from prying eyes.

Had Victoria always intended to have the children removed from the bastion of the royal grounds when they were able to withstand a distant journey? Did something unforeseen occur to change her thinking?

Did she weep and agonise over her decision? Did she have a choice?

Did the children who were no doubt also carrying the Scottish bloodline pose a serious threat?

I have also considered that whilst John Brown had (supposedly) passed away, it left Victoria without her support base and only the Brown family for protection. Whilst their progeny was a best kept secret, there was obvious knowledge and contention throughout the court and whilst Victoria was still Queen, there would have been less challenge to the children's existence or their presence on the Estate.

As some of Victoria's courtiers had a deep distaste and disrespect for the wild Ghillie John Brown they would have found it contemptable that their Queen had risked her status and health by giving birth to three heirs who now carried the mixed bloodline of the Scottish.

Their fate must have weighed heavily upon Victoria's shoulders. Knowing that forces were at play, how could it be ensured that those children were never to be recognised? How could they remain safely on British soil in their rightful domain?

Yes, it is a bizarre story. The rumours of their love affair and the long-muted suggestions that their liaison produced one or more children, seems to be vilified along with the information which I am now presenting.

This is Ursula's true account of her mother, Queen Victoria, and father, John Brown, and their 'other' three children, who are now their lost and forgotten families who became the Hobson line.

It is not a story of faint hearts. It is my grandmother's memoirs as told to me along with my observations throughout her long life. As you will read there is conjecture over the birth documentation for Ursula. On leaving England her bodyguard Eli Raycoft carried a Bible (same previously described by John Allen) with a date of 1884 written scantly in the front cover. This Bible was never found far from his bosom. It was as though that Bible was the one lasting link to their past. John and Annie had been chosen by Victoria as life protectors to ensure the future Royal line.

Annie Raycroft passed in Sydney in 1899 in her late thirties. Grandmother was only a very young girl. Annie's early death as Ursula's indomitable Nanny, governess and carer may have been one of the risks that the Royal House may not have factored.

The years dissolved any royal link. An unchallenged course of events occurred and the irrevocable decision to hide three children in a then isolated island called Australia. It is truly staggering how three children can disappear. Would Victoria be surprised at how well her plan played out but yet again would she have been astounded at the level of zeal which was kept? It is perhaps true that the three children had posed an issue; particularly as Albert's children had a vehement

Dedication

dislike for Victoria's relationship with John Brown and at every turn would revile their mixed bloodline brother and sisters. To have them cast aside was to be a blessing I can only assume. They also would take the secret to their graves.

This book gives insight into Ursula's strength of character, her steely determination and her family's secrets. It includes trials and tribulations which beset our family interspersed with touches of divine intervention which has always surrounded us and in freely attracting vital material fact and information to complete this book.

It has been a challenge; at times overwhelming to harbour the sensitive and presumptive nature of this information. I desperately wanted to scream these declarations and close the book before it was even opened. I felt troubled and compelled to talk to someone autonomous.

Thank you to the Hon. Peter Collins AM QC Managing Director Barton Deakin Government Relations for our meeting some 7 years ago at your office. I entrusted you with our story and I believe you were enthralled with my account and encouraged this book. This gave me further motivation, and importantly, comfort that you did not think I was a charlatan. Around the same time, I approached a popular television program suggesting the story would be of interest to their audience. My call was fobbed off very quickly.

A further approach was made to the office of a well-respected Australian director/producer and actor. I understand that this item is not your everyday topic but I always thought that reporters, directors and producers would have an open and enquiring mind (a 'nose') to at least query some of the information being dished up on a plate for them. To say that I was insulted is apt.

Along the way, being a busy and committed sole parent placed restrictions in fulfilling these ambitions due to the research time that was invested. It is a big and far reaching story. A story which needs a reverent and respectful approach. I have long kept my silence. During the last year if I have become remote to my friends and unavailable for a 'night at the movies' it is that I am compelled to complete this manuscript. It has become all engrossing and it has rightfully absorbed the majority of my time.

If this book is being held and read by other than a close few, I have achieved what I began many years ago and some amazing and dedicated publisher either has faith and trust in me and my family, or the foresight to publish it. In anticipation, thank you to my saviours for everything.

During this research, another amazing incident occurred which is unforgettable and is etched in my mind forever. I have prudently chosen not to share this incident. I am aware that the incident has also occurred to the royal family.

It is my hope that release of this book may unearth skeletons in musty archives or crypts laced with cobwebs. Even lost or secreted church records will give further credence and authenticity to these pages.

Based on the information that the children's minders, Annie and Eli were also in service at Cardiff Castle for The Marquis of Bute I made further representations in 1998. I didn't know that I had passed the incorrect information of the surname, being Allen and not Raycroft. Or perhaps they were both incorrect names used at the time of their tenure.

To Annie and Elias and their families, our deepest

thanks and gratitude for guarding with your own lives, my grandmother and her siblings, safely and dutifully until the time of your death. My heart aches as your descendants may still not know your final resting place.

Ursula's later life included an entourage of close and supportive friends here in Australia; the Bell family, Mr and Mrs Clarence Campbell, the families of Blair (who were related to the Farrell family), Hart, Smith, McLennan and Kinsela to name a few. You all shared and enjoyed the wonderful ritual of the Sunday roast or steak and kidney pie eaten heartily upon Nanna's Isle of Bute Castle crockery, including being treated to her culinary delight of lemon meringue, but you also provided her eternal friendship, love, and stemmed her loneliness…did you ALSO share her secret?

The Farrell name is significant in our family. My grandfather used this as his middle name. I am aware that my grandfather's mother Brigid had a maiden surname of Farrell. The Farrell family in the early 1900's owned and managed a haberdashery store in Newtown NSW of the same name.

My children…you are strong and always supportive

of me. I am very proud. Thank you for your values, your honour and being the quiet achievers.

Dad, I was blessed to spend memorable time together and perfect hours on your balcony discussing life, family and heritage affairs. I hope you are pleased.

Coincidentally, our family home remained so for most of my father's life in La Perouse New South Wales until 2002 and he spent the latter years by default on the banks of the Tweed River and then his last remaining year in our family home back in Sydney. Not knowing then that the Tweed River in England separates England from Scotland. How ironic.

To also discover that my aunty and uncle's home had been selected in Newport Sydney which is also the largest town in the centre of the Isle of Wight. Queen Victoria loved her Osborne House on the Isle off England's south coast. It seems feasible that three children could have certainly accompanied her majesty and John Brown during those holiday periods. Victoria also chose to spend her illness and eventual passing on these grounds in January 1901. Significant that her children endeavoured to commemorate those short memories of Newport, Braemar and La Perouse in respect of Victoria's love of the Italian and French coastline

We have also strangely lived for a period of time in Sandringham, Victoria.

Castle Life is Short Lived

'Turn around Peacock, turn around'. Ursula delighted in instructing the Peacocks to perform on the palace grounds by motioning them to turn in circles as their vivid colours spread into an elegant fan. Ursula lived on the palace grounds and would ride with her mother in their carriage.

I was a child but somehow spiritually connected on so many levels to my grandmother. Unbeknown to me, her life had taken a very different turn and there we sat; she in her eighties; an eternity from her home and cold deep waters separating truth and meaning.

Indelible in her mind was the horrendous sailing

journey which took place from England through Port Said to Australian shores. The voyage was to take many, many months and she recounted the putrid conditions, intense cold, incessant sheets of driving rain and what seemed a tiny vessel being pummelled against tortuous high seas. All aged in single figures, Ursula was the eldest child and both her brother William (Bill) and younger sister, Daphne were precious cargo.

Accompanying the infants were staunch royalists willing to spend a life of servitude for their Queen. Father and daughter Annie Raycroft[1] and Eli Raycroft[2], so nanna imparted. A large box of gold sovereigns, chattels and mementos also sailed half way across the world with them. Perhaps there was even a departing kiss, 'have a good journey dear ones.' There would be no return trip. Annie became ill onboard ship.

Their journey came to a thankful end and the clipper ship docked in Melbourne; perhaps not its preferred final destination due to Annie's illness.

Elias dutifully deposited the sovereigns into the

---

1   Queen Victoria's dresser and lady-in-waiting
2   The Black Rod in Parliament

Bank of New South Wales (Westpac?) and surely not through the teller machine! Initially the family settled into dwellings above a shop in Clarendon Street South Melbourne.

Shortly there was a run on the bank and they closed their doors. All of their savings were frozen (no bailout by the IMF here!) I can only assume a fortune was forever lost. The Alen or Allen children as they were now known were to face many more challenges.

The family then relocated to Sydney and must have resumed 'normal lives' until Annie died. Under these dire circumstances, Elias was not accustomed to 'women's work'. My father recalled that Elias stood tall, as did Annie, and would stand for no hi-jinx within the household. He used his cane to whirl in the air to command attention; particularly after Norman had duly kicked the cane from beneath his grasp and so pursued him doggedly down the hallway.

Ursula became an exemplary mother to the children as well as a dedicated sister in the ensuing years. She alone managed the tasks in the house and Eli was the security and financial maestro. No doubt the English Scottish-Australian pact had been cast and whatever occurred, could obviously not be rescinded. Aussies the children were to become.

My father Norman discussed that from a financial standpoint there was always strong regular support coming from England which maintained their fleet of vessels, and also assisted his parent's purchase of the matrimonial home. Mindful that William had not been a wealthy man prior to his marriage to Elsie Ursula. Although that support did not always continue from England.

Victoria's death in 1901 seemed to later impact greatly on our family. It seems that the pact to relocate to Australia did not leave any opportunity for seeking representation. Certainly no emails, faxes or telephone which could easily convey or discuss their future; particularly as circumstances had changed with the death of Annie.

Their relocation included a residence at 131 Oxford Street, Sydney above a ham and beef shop, or in today's terms, a butcher shop. Ursula (now commonly known to her friends as Elsie) was then to move to 'Rose Cottage' in Randwick (rear of the now racing stables). I am unsure where the name Elsie came from and why, but I have since been advised it is a short form of Elizabeth.

Ursula used the surname Raycroft Alen. Perhaps the link to the Raycroft's needed to remain as identification.

In view of those early conversations, knowing of the children's former years at the castle, I can categorically refute the accuracy of documentation which somehow was arranged to give legitimacy to having the children appear as being born in Australia. Particularly, her birth certificate details appear to have been overlayed. Notable is that the informant who supposedly attended Elsie's birth in Sydney was the name of John. England? This certificate certainly conflicts with her memoirs to me. But how difficult would it be for the Queen to organise these foils and keep a major secret? Not too difficult, I would think.

Father and daughter (as I had assumed), Elias and Annie appeared to have hailed from the Isle of Bute. It was gut wrenching that he should leave English shores and he openly cried to return to his homeland.

My understanding is that Ursula attended school at Lady Sacred Heart Kensington, New South Wales.

It is unclear what age she commenced. We have scant records for either Elsie's school years or her womanhood.

We would sit together on her bed. I brushed her thinning grey hair which crowned her small but determined face and I adorned her with Elizabeth Arden face cream and pearls. She gave me permission to trawl through her deep yellow oak dressing table (smelling strongly of freshly layered bee's wax) where three small drawers were located below the large mirror. It was like a Pandora's Box with excitement building as my small fingers scooped a myriad of special trinkets and smaller jewel boxes. I particularly admired and loved holding the brooch from Jimmy Pike[3]. This gift she wore constantly to secure her crisp cotton shirts at the neckline. Jimmy chose well, the horseshoe with riding crop encrusted with small diamonds and marquisites.

---

3   James Edward Pike nicknamed "The Master", was an Australian jockey who was known for riding Phar Lap to victory in the 1930 Melbourne Cup.
    Born: 4 September 1892, Newcastle **Died:** 7 October 1969, Bondi
    Nationality: Australian

I have since confirmed that Ursula's brother-in-law, Harold Page Douglass married to Daphne Victoria carried on a business of equestrian and saddlery. I feel that this may have been the connection to Jimmy.

My father told the story of their family friend, Jimmy Pike, the great Australian jockey who gifted a brooch to my grandmother. Jimmy Pike was also the first number-1 taxi plate holder in New South Wales. Jimmy surprised Ursula's daughter Ena with a pony which she duly named Dolly. Actually, Dolly clopped slowly behind Jimmy's taxi from Randwick to La Perouse. I suggest Dolly arrived many hours later and would have been exhausted.

Like two school girls, we chatted with no inhibition; she was forthright and sometimes abrupt and most definite in her ideas.

For years we enjoyed special time, sharing opinions, thoughts and smelling her lavender scented handkerchiefs which I passed to her to append her incessantly running nose. She certainly did not take well to winter and always wore layers of clothes. My father always suffered with this malady and intensely disliked the winter. He sometimes wore two to three pair of socks at one time stating that the years of constantly being saturated on board the fishing trawlers made his bones forever chilled! He never got warm.

Her bedroom was very large and a delight for a young girl. Thick shiny oak bedheads matching to her dresser. A small pretty alcove adorned with white fretwork and large casement windows where her favourite colour of wisteria fell softly in abundant shantung sheeting from copper rods and finials. Lead light windows of red, pale green and mauve dappled the sunlight softly onto the floorboards. Not ideal living on the coast her bedroom windows faced southward to Botany Bay and suffered the intense winds. Her room also captured the historic or what we children called the 'burnt house,' but which was originally the first Customs House in Australia.

The building had been occupied by Captain Arthur Phillip. Over the years the small but castle-like building became abandoned but had been rented to locals on several occasions. The last tenant had been climbing the spiralling sandstone staircase during the evening, carrying a lighted candle, which quickly caught fire to the curtaining. The residence was guttered. The tenant escaped unharmed as best as was described to me by my father.

Unbelievably artworks and frames were found charred amongst the sandstone ruins. These artworks had been painted by Arthur Phillip himself and had been concealed in the ceiling of the building. What a sad loss. As a child we played around the perimeter of that building collecting and making daisy chains for bracelets and necklaces. It remains today.

We talked of Chas. Pattinson (of the Soul Pattinson Chemist chain) with whom she was particularly smitten and who courted her and proposed marriage. It is now my belief that the powers that be also pre-ordained her future betrothal. At no point did she ever discuss with me any courtship with her husband William Farrell Hobson.

William Hobson and his family held substantial land in Maryborough Queensland. William at some point seemed to have hurriedly walked off those properties never to return. It is not known what happened to the land or the fate of the Kanakas working the fields. William curiously found his way to Sydney.

Captain William Hobson (1792-1842) first

Governor of New Zealand (and my father Norman William Hobson's great grandfather) was highly regarded by Victoria. As a successful Captain and pioneer and negotiator of the Treaty of Waitangi New Zealand he also named Hobson Bay in Canada and Hobson Bay in Melbourne Victoria a point of anchorage for his vessel. Captain Hobson's grave is located in Symonds Street Cemetery in Auckland New Zealand.

It is plausible that Victoria decided that her daughter would be well cared for by marrying into the Hobson family.

On March 16, 1912, William and Ursula were married at St. Georges Church, Paddington. This is also rather telling that most of the royals also marry in St. Georges Church London.

Ursula and William built their home which stood among one of the first private residences on the Peninsula of La Perouse. In those early days, La Perouse was isolated from the main Sydney hub. (From an archive I read it is also significant that Elsie Ursula's mother Victoria professed her love for one of her favourite retreats and restaurants along the Italian coast with the name of La Perouse). Also our loved home site until 2002.

Their Federation family home was solidly built with garage at left rear and rolling lawns which sloped upward to the backyard. Ursula's younger brother William lived with his sister and new brother-in-law William Farrell Hobson and enjoyed tending the gardens. He built two very large circular stone flower beds at the front which he kept meticulous with brightly coloured poppies and annuals. Unwittingly, his fate would end along these lines.

The front and main entrance to the house was approached from the south gate and guarded by two large pillars via a long pathway rising to a set of granite stairs and a veranda of rust/black/beige tessellated diamond shaped tiles. Either side of the stairway grew very large blue with mauve hydrangeas. On entering the hallway, you were met with picture rails of oak which had been extended from the wall to display a collection of ornate Indian pieces such as bells, timber figurines of Buddhas.. I also recall a very large circular bronze occasional table heavily designed and etched which was a feature of the vestibule and was placed on a black ebony base? These decorative items had travelled with gran from England.

The home site had been chosen overlooking the bay, mainly to give oversight to their vessels moored in Frenchman's Bay to the west. Frenchman's Bay had been named after Jean-Francoise de Galaup La Perouse whose monument was erected by the French Government. Compt. de La Perouse, due to bad weather conditions sailed into Botany Bay in his fleet of ships, 'La Boussole' and the 'L'Astrolabe" three days after James Cook who claimed the bay on behalf of the English.

The home site was a secondary choice as William had also purchased a parcel of land in Rose Bay located above where the flying boats operated passenger flights and the second parcel of acres where sits the Naval Base at Huskisson on the south coast of Sydney.

William also went on to purchase another three parcels of land in the same street as their newly built home in La Perouse.

Two Hobson family properties at La Perouse were built beside each other (my father built our family home in 1964, but sadly it has had several changes of ownership and has been substantially remodelled). Their close proximity made my visits to Gran often and easily. My very sporty parents June and Norman also made daily visits jumping the small white adjoining fence between our properties.

I have been miffed whether Nanna assessed me as being her closed lipped confidant or whether it was guilt or appeasement for having enticed my taste buds with a bottle of 'Blue Bow' lemonade which I found lying on the old laundry floor at the back of her property at the tender age of three.

The bottle contained Kerosene which was used to light the old copper on those dreary Monday mornings. It ignited the offcuts of wood piled in the cavity beneath the copper to stoke a fire enough to heat the water for a load of washing. It also ignited my tender lungs.

My recollection is sitting with nurse at the Prince Henry Hospital, Little Bay (only five minutes from home luckily) shoving some tube which felt half a football field long down my nose and throat pumping poison from my tiny stomach. Several weeks in intensive care I returned home delighted with my colouring books and pencils.

Those weeks of intensive care and the isolation from my parents (unable to visit me during those weeks and then only through the glass petition) for so long created many nightmares and sleepless nights for me.

I seriously believed that I had been left in an orphanage. Having sobbed uncontrollably every moment and so audibly, that my pillow was continually drenched. The policeman on duty at the hospital crossing, heard me and mentioned the "little girl crying all day" to my parents. My father was furious when he realised it was his daughter who was so distraught. He scooped me in his arms in bedsheets and took me home.

I suppose I saw him as my knight in shining armour. Over the years, thankfully hospitals have changed their policy and procedures in the treatment and convalescence of children.

The Hobson Line

I concluded in later years that the marriage between the Hobson family and Elsie Ursula had been pre-arranged by Victoria. Victoria's fondness and reliance on Captain William Hobson may have played a part in future management toward one of the ships fleet propelling three children into a new land. Ursula, Daphne and William would have arrived in Australia well before 17 July 1917, the date when the Saxe-Coburg family changed their names to Windsor. This may have been my grandmother's family name had she remained insitu. What was she christened at birth and on her real birth certificate prior to using Allen. What also of her siblings? The heirloom christening robe travelled with them from England and all of Ursula's children were blessed wearing this gown in the Church of England Randwick and probably also their grandchildren.

Elsie Ursula (Elsie as her friends called her) and her husband William seemed to have very little in common. Gran was a member of the Freemasons society and heavily involved in the Church. It was inherent that she be social, whereas William seemed so very disconnected with anything that did not involve being surrounded by nature, music or the sea. People did not overly interest him. He appeared to be searching for something more tangible in life.

William and his teenage son Norman spent weeks on their fishing boats, particularly those trips to New Zealand. They were rewarded with large caches of fish. As a seaman, William was very superstitious and wore the same navy surge jacket on every voyage. It seemed the same seagull would land its scrawny talons on the left side of his shoulder and leave his calling card. It was his good luck charm. It was a given that countless times William would interrupt the Sunday soiree with grandmother's friends by barging through the breakfast room wearing his trophy jacket caked with years of seagull residue. Elsie was reprimanded not to meddle in disturbing his luck however embarrassed she was.

William Clarence Raycroft Allen

U rsula said that Annie became ill on the voyage to Australia. Annie passed away in 1899 aged 37 leaving Eli to care for the siblings. Eli passed away aged 82 after being reluctantly cared for in a nursing home in Botany. It was his dying wish to return to England. For obvious reason that would never occur and particularly now that Victoria had passed in 1901.

Ursula's brother William (surname now Allen) worked for the Herald Newspaper in Broadway and his temper was hot! He was a type cast setter and remained at the establishment for many years.

William met Janet whilst working in Sydney and

were married. They celebrated the birth of their only son, John Allen.

Bill and Janet lived in Newport NSW where I visited once as a little girl. It was a stately looking home with large split level lawns at front held back by stone retaining walls. As previously mentioned, he was meticulous in his presentation and pride himself on his flower beds.

Bill and Janet were always visiting Ursula on the weekends and seemed very happy together. Unfortunately Bill did not live a long life. Janet was to hear a whirring sound coming from the front garden and alongside Bill on its side the wheels of the lawn mower still rotating. A fatal heart attack.

Again Ursula's heart was wounded and again her strength and resilience tested.

Daphne Victoria (Raycroft Allen) and Harold Douglass

My father Norman recounted many visits to the Douglass household at Brierley Street Cremorne NSW. (I have since learned that Council had rezoned the area which then became known as Mosman NSW).

My father related to me that after Annie had passed away Ursula struggled to care for the family and to run the household whilst still attending school. Eli made a difficult decision in having the youngest and the love of Ursula's life, her dearest Daphne, board with the wealthy Douglass Family. It is not known where that residence was situated. But it is now apparent that Daphne's friendship and love must have ignited during those early years with the Douglass clan or they may have even been betrothed through an arranged marriage. But we do know that they were immensely happy together until misfortune entered their lives.

Daphne and Harold Douglass did have a wonderful marriage and Norman loved to sit on his Aunt's lap whilst she told stories and twizzled his long blonde locks across his forehead. I did find a small postcard hidden in our Bible belonging to Eli. The postcard was written to her brother William on **May 21 (Monday) 1906.** She wrote sweetly and lovingly to him and asked him to be a good boy for his sister Elsie and to remind him that she would be coming to "tea" next Friday to visit them all at the La Perouse property and would stay the night until Saturday. Please pass this news on to their father. Why would you hide a postcard and why was it so important to be secreted within Eli's precious bible.

I must be missing something. I read, read again,

then studied this old sepic and fading postcard. **Of course, the date is ever so important.** The postcard is arrangement (a secret for their sister…(another secret Uugh!) for a pre celebratory birthday tea for Elsie! As our family had routinely enjoyed sharing gran's birthday on her mother Victoria's date of May 24. Signed off with lots of love from her loving sister always, Daphne. Eli was such an intelligent man. The postcard was the real key to the children's age. The date is the solver to the mystery. He was holding onto the truth in his special bible. The postcard then confirms my suspicion on the date of the journey from England to Australia. Confirmation they did sail from Plymouth as per the inscription in the front cover of the Bible of 1883 or 1884. So a monumental date.

Their Australian birth certificates **were** a foil. The postcard written by Daphne, having been written in 1906 shows exemplary penmanship and maturity and her text to Willie is way **too sophisticated for an 8 year old if the Australian birth certificates were accurate.** I would consider more in keeping with a woman of 18 or 20 years of age. Therefore I surmise her birth date would be 10 or even 12 years previous. What a big lie for them all! The **administration** applied this calculation to their certificates. Who would ever know?

Therefore the marriage certificate of Daphne and Harold Douglass certified that she was 20 years of age in 1914. So her birth year may really be around 1882 or earlier. So making her closer in age to her new husband Harold, aged 30 at their wedding.

Daphne was a fine woman.

Unfortunately Daphne and Harold were not blessed with children. Knowing that Daphne constantly indulged her nieces and nephews makes it all the more sad that they could have easily provided opportunities and a loving home had they shared a family together. Their home was situated nearby a small grocery and hardware store and Norman was always greeted with a new toy on his visits. Sometimes a model boat or Hornby toy train carriage on his birthday. Apparently Christmas was bliss at his Auntie's.

Ursula and Daphne were not only sisters but great friends and both cherished many hours together at their respective homes or enjoyed lunch and a Cinema

Tone afternoon in the city. They obviously shared much deeper secrets which bought them even closer together. Norman was always reluctant to depart Cremorne but Ursula dragged him to the local ferry stop at Mosman pier for the journey to Circular Quay and the bus home before dark beset.

Norman spoke so fondly of his loving Aunty Daph. He did recall that she had a portly figure. His recollection was also one of the tallest trees in Sydney metropolitan which grew in his Aunty and Uncle's Cremorne backyard. The tree could be seen from the Circular Quay Wharf. Their house was modest but comfortable and built on the high side of Brierley Street, but the garage was accessed from Spofforth Street where their vehicle was carefully backed out from the property. Their garden was also filled with flowers and apparently the Chrysanthemums were prolific with the heads so large that the stems were always drooping ground ward.

The front door was approached via a small pathway which opened to a hallway to reveal a very large English Grandfather clock which Harold ceremoniously and routinely wound.

Harold was a wealthy man, and from Norman's understanding, inherited a considerable fortune from his father. Including the saddlery and an equestrian and leather goods operation in North Sydney.

Harold was to fill his days in Sydney collecting rentals from all of his properties in and around Circular Quay and broader Sydney (nice work if you can get it!). Harold always drove the latest model cars and his favourite was the German built Studebaker.

Harold and Daphne Douglas also gifted a property in Wentworth Falls NSW to the Little Sisters of the Poor in Coogee. The land had been sub divided to include a small cottage which adjoined our family weekender not far from the station. The property had been in the family until very recently.

Harold was a jealous man and his love for Daphne impacted on Ursula's relationship with her sister. The hours spent shopping at Mark Foys and catching movies caused friction. He wanted the majority of Daphne's time.

An illness beset Daphne and she was swiftly admitted to hospital. Harold had visited Daphne during the day and was to return in the evening. On his approach through the ward he could see the white curtain drawn around Daph's bedside. Never had a man become so instantly maniacal. Daphne lay lifeless and Harold seized the doctor by the throat shaking with rage saying "you killed my wife".

Harold was never the same and became severely depressed. Ursula found it intolerable to have now lost her only sister and best friend. Harold had retreated from any routine or normality in his daily life. Visits to Brierley Street were few and far between as his health spiralled downward.

He slipped further into an abyss of depression without his beautiful Daphne. The home suffered from disrepair and Harold lost all sense of time. He sought to comfort his grief with copious amounts of alcohol. What was once a very dapper and well-respected businessman now became a piteous sight, as Norman, my father, caught a glimpse of his uncle some years later aimlessly walking Brierley Street wearing the same clothing with stains to his shirt and trousers. He was a rudderless ship now that his beloved had passed.

The grandfather clock stopped ticking and the

Studebaker had its last short jaunt as Harold, reeking of alcohol, backed out of the garage into the oncoming tram. Harold and Daphne were now together.

It is unclear what happened to Harold and Daphne's considerable estate. Norman's mother Ursula had expected that it would be left to her as next of kin. In 2012, Norman and I knocked on Brierley Street Cremorne. Uncannily he recognised the house and location but the house number had changed and the original number appeared at the other end of the street. The owners welcomed us in and Norman stepped back into his boyhood years pointing out the giant tree or rather the stump of the tree as it had now been lopped due to its size. Not a lot had changed and the owners were extremely surprised at his accurate recollections. We are still puzzled why the numbers in the street had changed and been reversed.

William Farrell Hobson

10 SEPTEMBER 1888 TO FEBRUARY 1958

My brief recollections of Coogee Aquarium was the strong odour of chlorine due to the lack of ventilation in the old pool building. The pool was not of the Olympic ilk and the tiers of dark wood seating/galleries were constructed high above the pool similar to an amphitheatre where thundering cheer squads could enjoy the racing youngsters. Ashamedly, today it would surely be heritage listed. The entrance to the pool was through the old turnstiles and timber slats covered the tiles to avoid slipping.

As a young school girl, swimming carnivals were generally held at Sunstrip Pool (known as Wylies

Baths) or Coogee Aquarium. Later the Dawn Fraser Municipal Pool was to become the more modern and popular choice for the events. As a very young girl, I was unaware that my family owned the Aquarium when I swam. My lovely friend Joanna who also lived and attended school in Randwick also shares my love of the Coogee Aquarium and we love to share our memories of our primary school days swimming the carefree sports-days away.

Grandfather Bill was a wonderful freestyle swimmer. His associations included the esteemed swimmers of Wickham and Keiran who together trained and competed at the old baths.

He won copious races and was scheduled to tour the world with Theodore Tartakova (dual Olympian swimmer 1908 London and 1912 Stockholm) with an exhibition of the Australian Crawl, but the Black Plague through London and Europe halted that. It seemed a true contradiction that Elsie had a total dislike for boats and particularly the water, but she also could not swim. What a risk considering their journey to Australia!

Living in Melbourne in my single days, I attended a

function with a friend which coincided with the commencement of the ARL Football season. There were some great and well-respected footballers and coaches at the event and it was a fun evening and a chance encounter with one of my distant relations. I was unaware that somewhere along the line the Giles family and Mina Wylie were connected to our Hobson family. Although it would account for their wonderful swimming prowess. So many important matters and information has long been overlooked and unrecorded. What lament when you suddenly realise it is too late to capture those significant milestones. They will remain buried.

I can only urge families to consider documenting their family tree earlier rather than later and savour precious moments that may pass without recognition. It was a blessing to have had a great friendship with my gran; listening intently to her fantastic life and now it results in a tangible document to leave for my family and those families still yet to follow.

William Farrell Hobson (my grandfather) had three brothers; Charles, Albert, William and sisters Beatrice (Beattie), Margaret (Maggie) and Nina (Nin). William Farrell's father was Charles William Hobson (they called him "Old Hobbie" and his mother Bridget Agnes Farrell.

Old Hobbie obviously was a war veteran as his proud memento was a Russian metal war helmet which ominously displayed a bullet hole straight through the centre at forehead level. Apparently the antique was significant for him and he always held that helmet close to his chest.

Although my grandfather William had been groomed as a lawyer in the firm of Rand & Drew, he and his brother Charlie also found time to be credited with improving Fanny Durack's swimming stroke. During the winter months, the Aquarium baths were converted into an ice rink and Bill played piano whilst couples romanced the evening away to the wee hours. Bill played piano by ear and would be an avid cinema buff – his favourite movies 'Laurel and Hardy' which had him laughing even after the show. Bill also loved his musicals and would re-create the classics on his return home. He mostly did not need sheet music.

Included in the Coogee ice rink was a switchback which allowed the more athletic and proficient skaters to perform jumps and aerial manoeuvres. My father's uncle, Ronald Hobson was the expert in crafting and sharpening the blades and would be responsible for the upkeep of the boots for the patrons. As I best understand Ronnie excelled in the engineering field and his family have continued his successful legacy. It was marvellous to have eventually spoken to them by phone for the first time.

The Sydney to Hobart yacht races record shows Ronnie Hobson had significant prowess as a sailor and captained two wins in the renowned yacht race; as my best understanding in the yachts, 'Joanne Brody' and 'The Ripple'. He also held office as the Commodore of the Cruising Yacht Club, Rose Bay in Sydney.

The Coogee Aquarium was the first retailer to import Cadbury chocolates into Australia and the featured tins were one of the best sellers at the baths. It was also grandfather Bill's downfall. His sweet tooth pressured him into devouring a kilo of chocolates prior to breakfast!

Hobson Court was adjoining the swimming baths and was also a block of flats which still remains today. The venues became a social hub in Coogee and was known as 'The Club'. Conversely, the 'Coach & Horses

Hotel' in Randwick was another popular social venue for him and his swimming club members.

Grandfather William Hobson was a born seaman (as the salt running through the veins of his grandfather) and at every opportunity he would exit the family baths to find solace on the ocean waves in his large seagoing vessel then moored in Rose Bay. He was a free spirit. The ocean was a world away from the social etiquettes of lawyers, society people and the habitual cleaning and maintenance of the baths and public amenities demanded of their operation. Particularly the bathing towels which were then part of the bathing experience, became burdensome as no clothes dryers had yet been invented. Inclement weather certainly bought with it excess pressures to find ways to dry, fold, and rack fresh towels at the entrance turnstile along with the locker keys.

In those early days, the majority of bathers were male and very few women wanted to abandon the 'modesty' label except Fanny Durack would appear in the baths in a 'neck-to-knee' bathing costume. Ms Durack ignored the male members of the baths and their whispers and not looking right or left, no discussions, proceeded with business and her Olympic dreams; dived in, swam her laps and exited the baths as quickly as she had entered. Apparently the male members of the baths in respect did not enter the water whilst she was training.

William approached his father to propose what we would call a 'realignment' in his career. He wanted 'out 'of the baths and professed that a practising lawyer was certainly not what he himself wanted from life but a life on the seas. Old Hobbie was very angry and adamant that if Billy chose this direction he would be certainly cut off without a penny.

It is unsure how William and Ursula were introduced. Gran never discussed this information with me needless to say that she spent a lot of time helping out at the baths prior to their marriage.

Despite his father's previous warning to pursue his law studies, William seemed strangely flushed with funds and as previously disclosed purchased several parcels of land.

One of these parcels of land had been chosen to design and erect a family home which overlooked Frenchman's Bay, then a secluded beach enclave tucked away from the ravaging winds which blew unforgivingly from the Pacific Ocean through the heads of Botany Bay.

William's life seemed to have changed dramatically and so did his fortune. He must have formulated many plans; firstly to start a family and secondly as a Shipwright to craft large fishing vessels. Bill purchased a very large boatshed on the shores of Frenchman's Bay.

My father Norman Hobson in MV 'Miss Flash' conveying passengers foreshore Frenchmans Bay La Perouse to Kurnell.

Ena Ursula Hobson

BORN 4.01.1912

The first child born to Ursula (Elsie) and William Hobson was a very pretty blonde, blue eyed daughter. The couple chose to name her Ena Ursula. She was Bill's pride and joy. My aunty was intelligent and she had a wonderful outgoing personality. We loved sharing Christmas Day with her. She at the helm, baking the Christmas dinner in unison with my mother and gran. She was bubbly and as my father informed me she had held a significant role as a private secretary in the ministry of J.T. Lang. Ena was similar to Gran in that they were wonderful hostesses.

John (Jack) Allen Hobson

BORN 24.01.1925

Jack was the last of the children born to William and Ursula. Jack was the tallest of the boys and was to become a successful industrial chemist and director on several boards. Jack is also a learned man and is proficient in several languages. Both brothers shared a yearning for independence and needed no bolster of company; they were self-made men and tough.

Norman William Hobson

BORN 29.04.1916

Norman was the second born child of William and Elsie Ursula Hobson. A home birth for his mother who was in labour for three days, mainly due to my father being an extremely large baby and a New South Wales state record weighing in at 14 lbs (one stone) in the old scale.

Norman was a lean frame and mostly never weighed more than 65 kg which well and truly belied his birth weight. He was a natural cricketer and was selected for the A team at Sydney Technical High School. The boys were raised in the frenzy and greatness of Sir Donald Bradman and they were chosen to represent the school to bowl and bat to the real Don Bradman at the Moore Park location opposite Sydney Boys High School. Norman also went on to purchase a Bradman bat which the great sportsman autographed for my father. How fantastic. Norman went on to play many more interschool games into his teen years until he became interested in sculling and joined a rowing eight.

He tired of the journeys from La Perouse to Haberfield several times a week for training which usually resulted in one or more of the rowing eight failing to attend. His insistence in being totally independent lead him to canvas the single scull discipline which gave him the option to sometimes train at Frenchman's Bay when the weather permitted.

He became so enthralled with the sport that after his first purchase of a rowing shell he built his own craft which duly served him to win 16 NSW Championships undefeated. He refused to race during the war years so there was a gap between those championship years. My father was a perfectionist and did not attempt anything half-hearted. His greatest ambition was to represent Australia at the Olympics. A dream which was not realised due to there being rules permitting heavyweight scullers only to represent Australia. It is now certainly a changed sport and there is certainly a light weight category for competitions. Particularly the romance of the beautiful timber boats which gave way to Kevlar and other such lightweight craft. He was no advocate of any material which was not sound, including the change in design of some of the blades (sculls, oars) on the market.

Certainly not a heavyweight, he changed his diet to bulk up to well over 12 stone however, his results were far less spontaneous in his races; his muscles were used to quick recoil and the extra weight burdened his muscle reactions. In a short amount of time his body shed the extra poundage.

His rowing colleague at times was Mervyn Wood who represented Australia as the heavyweight singles sculler at the Olympics on the Skykyl River in Germany. On his return, Mervyn was kind in revealing that based on race times, there was no one in the world that could have beaten Norman as a lightweight sculler.

Father was an athlete and a health stalwart even in those early days and was always interested in starting his own gymnasium with mother. As a boy he would train by running in the early mornings prior to daylight to avoid the embarrassment of being seen. He was a non-smoker and drinker but never stopped exercising. He still had a very sporty physique even at 97, maintaining muscle mass in his arms which did justice to the anchor tattoo displayed on his upper arm.

During the 70's, one of the tools he developed and designed was a complex looking rowing machine with many little dials which calculated the rates per minute and the pulling power plus other information in one single rowing movement. This assisted in the continual improvement of his performances. He was also friends with and became engrossed with the work of the very intelligent Professor Cotton who was even in those early days trying to improve the rowing technique. I believe the Professor was a sports physiologist and ergonomics expert and the two like minds always questioned why things were done as routinely as they were.

Father offered his coaching services to many of the GPS schools, including St. Josephs School, Newington and Kings School. My father was a carpenter, engineer, building trades foreman, rigger, designer and shipwright and a work study expert and always found ways of improving all that he did in life. He loved to succeed and challenged himself at every turn. I loved the way he was so analytical and saw things differently to other people. He often wore a buffed sharks tooth on a leather lace around his neck.

Together he and his father William began building boats on their vacant adjoining block to the family home at La Perouse. They produced some very large boats; some 100-foot-long and when the time came for it to be launched, an entourage heralded by a large jinker was engaged to assist in its lifting for the journey to Rose Bay. In those days, the whole process was captured on Cinema tone movies at the local theatres. One boat in particular was The Nella Tub which was sold to the McLeod family in Timaru, New Zealand. I am sure she is still in good working condition and would love to visit her sometime.

It was Norman and his father's intention to continue

in the wholesale supply of fish and seafood but things were to change significantly for the family.

What was the secret lodge and the "rendezvous" which occurred often on a Tuesday evening? Both my father and his brother Jack and Ursula seemed to head in the same direction in their car. On these occasions they carried a rectangular suitcase which I found open and witnessed a ceremonial apron used routinely at their meets. Apparently, a coveted organisation which is entered by way of invitation or network. As I have read, this order is hundreds of years old and can be traced back to pagan times. Father would not discuss these meetings.

Lady Ursula

She swivelled slowly from her large bed which dwarfed her tiny frame. Her tight luminous well-worn hands and long fingers grasped for her floral cotton housecoat which always lay on the crimson pink occasional chair. The bedside table held a night lamp and a cream squat Bakelite radio whose face lit a golden yellow. Its several knobs and dials were always appealing to quickly change the channels to create a mixture of muffled voices and sounds to make you laugh.

Nanna's travel clock sat in its own little case as a turtle-in-a-shell. That clock had shared much of my grandmother's long life. It was always watching her in sleep.

Those shared moments in the early 1960's are now

cemented in my mind because they bought us so very close together. My grandmother loved me and trusted me. She could be herself and she could let go. We had a few laughs – not too many as she was mostly serious and austere.

That clock was a real task master – the morning ritual began with the boudoir – the dressing room. Her real silk undergarments usually the palest of pink sat over her torsolette or girdle – a leftover ancient femme fatale which pulled the waistline into an hour-glass curve. The silk stockings were guided slowly over her feet and ankles to cover her spindly legs. It was then that time stood still. Less than dextrous fingers always struggled where hose met the metal stays. I would assist by tightening the "strangle hold" between the two opposing parties.

She would give instructions as to the colour and denier of the next purchase of stockings. The denier was to be neither too thick nor too thin and maintain a 'tanned' look to disguise the lily whites. The silks were purchased usually at Mark Foys, the biggest of the department stores in those days in Sydney and then Farmers. They would arrive home in a beautiful shiny box – silks were expensive and popular with those early beauty actresses. During the war years it was cheap and fashionable for women to colour their legs in tan and hand draw a black seam at the back of the leg in simulation of the real thing.

There was not a great variance in her daily wardrobe, as she mainly chose the plain navy mid-length skirt, but there was an array of beautiful blouses of cotton and plaid with either Swiss Voile with a frilled bodice, a jabot (at the neck) or Jimmy's brooch which would sit holding the neckline together.

To the bathroom we would trot where her short and neat greying hair was beaten into submission by copious amounts of water run through with a hair comb. Her hair held body and was swept in an upward motion similar to her daughter Ena's style. We would then journey to the small but sun-filled breakfast room which adjoined the sun room and the compact but functional kitchen with fuel stove. Her joy was the soft-boiled egg with rounds of toast which was completed by jam or honey and butter accompanied by a pot of steamy tea which was coddled by a tea cosy. Let the tea settle for a few minutes – turn the pot around twice and pour.

My grandparents, the Hobson's, were prolific socialisers and entertainers. Having been in the hub of Randwick and Coogee in the 1900's, it had been Elsie Ursula's disappointment to relocate to La Perouse such a duration away from Sydney town. When not building ocean-going vessels, William was on the high seas or having business enterprises in New Zealand. Not only was the Hobson home a ritual for her friends on a Sunday, but they joined her for holidays at the Chalker Estate in Braemar south of Sydney, not far from Bowral. My father recollected those boundless and carefree school holidays on this property. Ursula mentioned that her father had been presented with a silver cup for tossing the Caber at the Braemar Games in England.

As a small boy, my father loved being collected by the Chalker family at the train station in those early years by a pony and trap. Access was made via a sandy laneway across a small bridge. Recalling his delight driving beneath the spell of the green canopy of ancient trees which laden with cold dew drops fell onto his school cap and across his brow. He also spoke of playing with his sister in the wool wash close by the house.

Mrs Chalker was renowned for preparing hearty nutritious meals and apple pies with churned cream made lovingly in her country kitchen.

It was at this holiday accommodation that my grandmother played tennis and was king-hit on the nose. A trip to the doctor holding her very swollen face revealed a broken nose. Obvious from the photograph below. Not her best look. Therefore, accenting the German 'Saxe Coburg' noses that the family already had inherited so prominently.

Cold Deep Waters

TRYING TO PUT THINGS INTO PERSPECTIVE

As a child it was not evident that I would be the recipient of information, stories, names and events which would eventually become an obsession in piecing together our family's history and the link across cold deep waters.

Certainly conflicting information which greatly differed from dubious documentation such as their birth certificates bearing new christian and surnames which would attach to them for the remainder of their lives.

A coup of such advanced and divisive planning. Only at that top level were those plans able to succeed. My family had no doubt been cautioned to remain with sealed lips.

To spirit three children and their carers around the world to another country without being missed is truly bizarre. But its success and risk had no doubt been determined and executed so well to the last detail. Perhaps those loving families who were left behind, knew that their betrayal of the events would be treasonous.

In any event, this secret was a resounding success. Perhaps too successful. It is on a personal level and with mixed emotions that as these revelations are disclosed I am now breaking a zeal. But as many would say the 'old England is gone forever'.

Children left behind on a cold winter shore, perhaps in darkest night, all now passed on with never the opportunity of being re-united with their relatives. Perhaps that will change after this book has been published and I look forward to those re-associations.

I also write honestly and with pleasure to finally lift the obvious burden placed on my grandmother and her siblings Daphne and Bill. Also in respect for Annie and Eli Raycroft and their family and ancestors who would not have known of their final resting place.

The information entrusted to me and the mystery story became a vow to my father. It is this promise now honoured. The information contains material facts based upon my witnessing the last recording of Princess Alice of Althone made at around age 90. Facially, she and Gran could have been twins. Also the posture, countenance, hair and every inch no doubt sealed that my grandmother was most assuredly, part of the Royal family.

It is not known in which vessel the family were

transported to Australia. As I have read that Lord Melbourne was in regular attendance in Victoria's Court, it seems plausible that he may have recommended the destination of Melbourne as being far enough away to be suitable.

Victoria's *secret* was to ensure the safety and longevity of her children and to relocate them to a faraway land. To successfully legitimise their new lives would not have been too difficult a task and it goes without saying that Victoria was easily able to open doors without contention.

Of significance, my father recalls a gold snake bracelet encrusted with emeralds which was gifted to Gran Ursula through Annie. I was to inherit a tiny fine delicate purse perfume bottle. Also a very small antique fan with a frame of ebony passed on by John Brown. I was told the tiny item was used by the courtesan to pencil the name of the suitor for their next dance. John was the favoured MC at those dances

Through Eli, the purse sized fan carried with it a perpetual family message. Should our family be in any trouble, we were to present the fan back to the Castle. Ursula's daughter Ena did just that many years ago. She journeyed to Cardiff Castle with the antique piece. No one recognised it. My thoughts are that it was taken to the wrong castle (as you do). Perhaps it was meant for Buckingham Palace.

We have a Coronation journal 1935 and a Peerage journal which unfortunately was stolen.

Curiously I have also found in our storage an old woollen-style square of blanket which is brown in colour on one side and red tartan on reverse. The blanket is not soft but harsh to the touch and the ends are badly frayed. Both sides are entirely a different pattern. It is noted from the very few official photographs of John Brown in his kilt there is a strong similarity to the cape or sash which crosses his shoulders.

Another of my prized possessions is a sextant which I am told was passed from Captain William Hobson through the family which has the hallmark manufacture of Henry Hughes and Son, Fenchurch Street London (Marine Opticians).

On the marriage of Ursula and William, her sister Daphne was witness and it is noticeable that both women signed Raycroft with a long keystroke over the R, as for Regis. Also of interest is that Ursula's daughter was christened Ena. All of my female cousins appear to be linked by name. Even though Victoria at some stage took the decision not to promote her Christian name it would not be unreasonable to assume that these names are a derivation of Alexandrina as well as Linda. Alen also satisfies the possibility of a derivation of Victoria's Christian name used as the children's surname.

My understanding from Ursula was that Annie was not married. (Perhaps there was a requirement that all of the lady's-in-waiting were not to be married?) Even though documents suggest otherwise. It has to be wrong. It is my hope that the Church of England may have been entrusted with some of Victoria's documents. Also it is my deepest desire that Victoria may have also left some communication or parting gesture to Ursula and her siblings should the secret or pact be broken?

Was it Victoria's intention to cut ties **completely** on that dark monumental voyage from Plymouth? Why was the distance factor between Australia and England so imperative? Presumably there was no consideration to continue raising the children on British soil.

There seemed a considerate side to Victoria having

capitulated by sanctioning marriage between Princess Louise and the Duke of Argyle, John Campbell. Princess Louise had many of her own interests in painting and the arts and she was least interested in marrying into royalty contrary to her mother's wishes and in broadening the royal house. This was definitely a deviation and would have been known as a landmark decision.

But I do know most definitely this plot could not have succeeded without the key players. Many assumptions and probabilities have been raised by authors, researchers and persons attesting their links and right to royal passage. I declare none so detailed as one who has spoken and had an ongoing relationship with Victoria's daughter.

As previously confirmed and discussed with Grandmother Ursula, Victoria had married John Brown in a clandestine service with Annie presiding over the ceremony. Among the inscription in Eli's Bible is a list of names… some even sign with an 'X' Significant is the copperplate initials 'WF' which is the focal point. I can only assume that was the consecration of the marriage ceremony and/or their departures?

My heart aches for both Annie and Eli who gave up their lives at home in Bute for dutiful loyalty and service to Victoria. What was of interest is that when both Annie and Eli passed away they were interred together in a completely different section of the cemetery to Ursula without markings or gravestones.

A momentous occasion caught when Nella was finally ready to be jinkered for launch to Rose Bay mooring No.1. Norman raises his hat in exhaultaton!

Always the very proud and upright Norman at 93 years.

Always pensive Norman at age 93.

Arriving at Rose Bay by jinker ready for launching.

Author forefront of the La Perouse monument of Compt. de La Perouse.

Bare Island Fort Musem. Active in the Boer War.

Blanket assumed to have been used by John Brown at La Perouse.

Crowd at scene of Congwong Bay, La Perouse 2000 Olympics. Torch bearing relay leg. Olympian Mervyn Wood torchbearer.

Dad at 80 having fun with Ben his dog.

Elsie Ursula Allen Hobson with family.

Elsie Ursula Raycrof Allen birth certificate created here in Sydney.

Elsie Ursula and her sons Norman and Jack at their sister Ena's wedding.

Elsie Ursula with her family.

Elsie Ursula dressed for an outing in Sydney NSW. Boat building in progress behind.

Elsie Ursula in the streets of Sydney NSW.

Father always not far from the water. Tweed NSW.

Elsie Ursula one of our many joyous Christmases.

Elsie Ursula's first and only car sitting at La Perouse home. Her licence given at the age of 72.

Jack Hobson the tall one in centre at a family function.

Excitement builds in the street as the vessel is transport ready.

First Customs House in Australia.

Grandfather William Hobson presentation of swimming trophies.

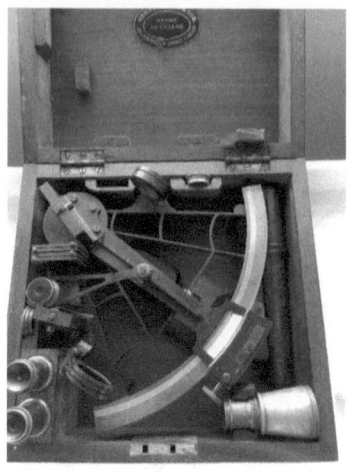

Heirloom Sextant of Cptn. William Hobson my great grandfather.

Marketing of the first parcels of land at La Perouse.

Image of the La Perouse reserve where boomerang throwing occurred for tourists. Opposite Congwong Bay and in foreground the prestigous NSW Golf Club.

John Brown.

June on her wedding day.

John Brown's precious Bible.

Marriage Certificate Elsie Ursula to William Hobson 16 March 1912 St.Georges Church, Paddington NSW.

Momument to Compt. de La Perouse.

My aunty Ena and Elsie Ursula's first daughter.

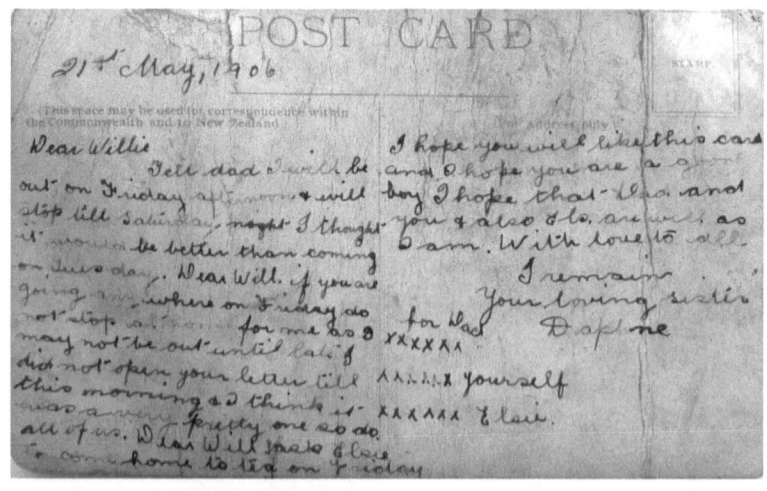

My aunty Daphne's postcard found secreted in Eli' (John Brown) Bible.

My father Norman at the age of 6 dressed for a pantomine as an angel.

My mother June Evans Hobson.

Norman Hobson in his early 20's preparing for a race at Leichhardt Rowing Club.

Norman Hobson with his dog Robbie the Daschund.

Norman William Hobson as Foreman at ICIANZ Matraville NSW Australia.

Norman and brother Jack.

Norman as a young teenager in Sydney working for the Vacuum Oil Company in Margaret Street.

Norman looking very debonair at La Perouse NSW.

Norman middle row third from right sitting proudly in his school football team 1933.

Norman on his way to work in Sydney NSW.

Norman training upper Nepean River NSW outside Fallicks Cave. About 32 years of age.

On of the large craft being built beside the La Perouse residence. William Hobson and sons Norman and Jack as teenagers.

One of the Hobson vessels moored at Rose Bay NSW.

One of the first buildings in La Perouse was the Salvation Army home now the La Perouse Museum overlooking Frenchmans Bay.

Paragon restaurant in 1974 devastated at La Perouse.png

Photograph taken of a rare collision at sea by Norman and his father William. Unknown vessels.

My Grandmother Elsie Ursula with her brother William Clarence

Sextant heirloom passed from Cptn. William Hobson, First Governor of New Zealand.

Sextant box.

> 22-11-54
>
> 27 Cain St,
> Timaru,
> Nth. Canterbury
>
> Dear Mr. Hobson,
>
> I am sorry I have been so long in sending these snaps. I hope they will be what you'd like to see. A day or so after I had your letter "NELLA" came in with 100 cases of fish on board, the first time ever. She has had 99 and + once 85. Is "LLENA" sold yet? If so I expect you would feel quite upset to see her go.
>
> Although it is a little previous, I'll close now & wish you & your family a Merry Xmas & Happy New Year.
>
> With kindest regards
> Yours truly,
> Elsie McLeod.

Rare photograph of grandfather William Hobson doing business in New Zealand with Cpt. Langley, Mr Cain and Cptn. McLeod. Sent as tribute along with a heartfelt letter on the passing of William.

The La Perouse residence early 1900's adjoining block where the ship's such as Nella were built. Notice electricty stantion behind Hobson residence.

The athletic William Hobson, great swimmer and proprietor of the Coogee Aquarium, Coogee NSW.

The author aged 9 sitting at the front of souvenier shop La Perouse with a beloved toy Kangaroo.

The grave of Compt. de La Perouse.

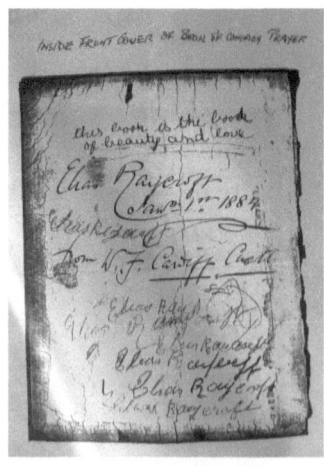

The Bible carried by John Brown with inscriptions on inside of cover.

The old bridge connecting La Perouse to Bare Island.

The parapet and walled garden of Cardiff Castle, Wales UK in September 1998 our eerie visit never forgotten.

The wheel house of the Nella Tub.

John Brown with stag.

William Hobson climbing the ladder of success.

William Hobson with his family overshadowing the dimunitive La Perouse behind in the newly built Nella.

John Brown the Scot.

John Brown in dinner suit.

John Brown standing in arch.

Secrets, Castle Conversations and Deja Vu

In 1998 I visited Cardiff Castle. I knew from the stories given to me by gran that she had a connection with the castle and that Annie had been in service there with the family as lady in waiting for Victoria. What a very different world they must have experienced at the castle until their final transition to Australia.

The following guarded conversations and happenings at the Castle were passed down from Annie to Ursula and then to me:

The Marquis of Bute was going through periods of

serious concern and reflections of his life. Back and forth he would pace with his hands folded behind his back. This was to continue over many weeks. It was one staffer who felt concern for the Marquis. It would have been well out of the gentleman's station in life to address his Lordship but he must have sensed the growing burden upon his shoulders and could not help himself but enquire of his Lordship's dilemma. To this, his Lordship responded that the gentleman was the only one that had cared to approach his Lordship to offer assistance and comfort. The Marquis duly granted the gentleman a large parcel of land freehold for his trouble.

Annie was also to overhear the Marquis again pacing, pacing; rambling to himself, "with all my money I cannot save myself". The Marquis at that time found out that he was suffering an illness. He realised that money did not satisfy all of life's upheavals.

The excitement peaked when I entered the walled roof garden in the tower which is surrounded by the castle parapet. The family had discussed the roof garden many times and Ursula knew of the tree which grew in a table. As well the secret tunnel, but it is best that secrets remain so. The schedule of visits by the royal family between the castles in winter and summer is not clear, so I assume that Annie also travelled between them with Victoria during these seasons.

My whole body tingled as the strangest Deja vu feeling came over me that I had been there before in that castle and that gripping connection made me not wanting to leave...I would have been content to stay forever. It was like coming home. We joined a small tour who had positioned themselves standing and sitting around the garden walls of the parapet to listen to the tour guide. We found a seat in one of the very well-worn stone alcoves with stone seating which had been designed around one side of the room. Each cubicle was interspersed with quaint little flipper-type windows which were well locked.

Within the first few minutes of the session an incredible roar was heard surrounding the castle. It was so loud that it was deafening. The guide and the group remained still and silent. I listened to its howl as it seemed to travel around the parapet and it was to end with my daughter and myself.

The locked flipper window beside the two of us

burst open and that deafening noise pushed past our shoulders, head and neck. It was one of the earie things in life. Inexplicable. There was someone who wanted us to know they knew we were in the castle. An unforgettable moment. I am sure the guide will remember as we discussed the fact that I had relatives that had worked at the castle… but I did not elaborate. I enquired of the treed table to which he replied was taken to the basement many years ago and how did I become aware?

For the remainder of the afternoon I was enthralled with the Great Hall and the gigantic open hearth which must have held some wonderful roaring fires whilst all enjoyed an evening of fun and dance.

I pictured John Brown organising dances as the Master of Ceremonies in his finest kilt and downing a few scotches as he was known.

Ursula also had mentioned 'the keep' which stood in a central location immediately viewed from the castle gates on entrance. It is somewhat larger than I had thought. The keep was to hold all of the meat and produce for the castle.

<u>I shall return to that Castle.</u>

Life in an Idyllic Coastal Village

Our small coastal village was pristine in those early days. Isolated apart from the purpose built Salvation Army home which sat dominantly overlooking Frenchman's Bay. The bay was remote and the terminus stop for the tram where it circled, collected passengers and returned to Sydney city. There was also on the opposite end of the Bay a very large home or mansion-like structure built by an English ship's captain in the early days. Those two buildings majorly flanked the small bay. Otherwise few homes occupied the small hamlet. Some Aboriginal families lived behind the idyllic beach and on a weekend they would sell their beautifully crafted and engraved boomerangs, shell encrusted jewel boxes with silk linings, Nulla Nulla's and beaded jewellery. One famous local family, The Timbery's Joe and Marjorie, were regarded as the royals of the Aboriginals. More than one Sunday as a young girl I joined Charlie Pender, who was a great boomerang exponent who spent his weekends promoting the aboriginal culture in throwing the boomerangs for and with the tourists. There is ABC footage taken on one such occasion with both of us explaining the ancient art (me with plaits and all). Charlie would delight the crowd throwing two Boomerangs simultaneously and catching both on their return.

Small humpies and makeshift dwellings dominated the landscape in Happy Valley overlooking Congwong Bay on the opposite side to Frenchman's Bay throughout the war years. It was home for many years to destitute families throughout the depression years.

My grandfather William was an old-fashioned gentleman where a woman's place was as a homemaker and mother. Ursula did not fall into that mould exactly. She took control of the family home extremely well.

Ursula was busy raising two sons and her eldest

daughter Ena; mainly due to her husband William always being on board boat. Grappling with the loads of washing in the outside laundry where the old copper would be stoked with wood and kerosene (and empty lemonade bottles!) until the boiling water had peaked and a clump of 'blue bag' was added to keep the whites crisp and whiter again. She would then use a wooden prod or stick to open the copper lid and twirl and twist the materials to stop tangles and make sure all of the clothes were fully immersed in water.

This process occurred weekly until the Hills Hoist was ceremoniously and excitedly erected in the backyard years later. Prior to this, the old rope line with two or three props held the washing in position of the sun (and wind) until the southerly wind sprang up and the props would fall leaving the washing in a clump to the ground. It was only white linen in those days. As there was no spinning mechanism involved in the weekly washing, the sodden clump lay lifeless in the old wicker basket until the inclement weather had passed or indeed if it was severely bad weather, they would be returned through that gruelling process once again.

In the 1950's there was always local domestic help seeking to add to the weekly family income and Ursula employed several women over the years to dust, vacuum (prior to the electric vacuum the old Bissell push floor type model.) The iron was also not electric but heated on an iron pad.

Considering the largeness of the available land in our suburb it was staggering that Ursula met with clanging and hammering beside the large vacant nature strip alongside the family home. The Sydney County Council (I think) had decided to erect the first electric transformer beside the house. The pole driver was thundering the large metal stanchions and frames into the ground. The structure stood taller than the house.

This lady was enraged and meant business as she flew out of the back door to connect with the foreman explaining that she was not standing for this monstrosity and to re-locate it. He replied that he had orders madam. Not responding to his tone, she raced for the old black Bakelite phone (her number was FJ 5090) and asked the operator for the electric company number. She had some pull that woman. By late afternoon a representative was at her home and the transformer was to be disassembled and re-located. Meanwhile Bill was on the high seas. Just another day.

My father Norman, as a child, was also an adventurer and enjoyed making tin boats and sailing them in the Bay. A number of his local friends-in-crime also shared his curiosity and fun. George Rogers, Billy Fisher, Ronnie Chiltern and Bobby Simms to name a few. The boys were to dare each other. I was told that one of the boys decided to climb a massive crane- like piece of equipment which floated on a huge pontoon off the shoreline and which was used for transferring anchors and tackle between the vessels. The crane stood around 30 feet in height.

The bravest (or silliest) shinned up the crane like a

monkey. As he climbed further skyward the boys' jibes and jokes subsided when the enormity of that prank had settled on them. There was deathly silence. The shivering monkey was to turn and look below, losing his confidence and more importantly his grip – he hurtled to an abrupt stop. He did not move. Norman and his friends were too scared to look. He was coiled in ropes at the base of the structure which had protected the worst of his fall. The monkey awoke groggy and very sore. They hightailed it out of the crime scene. An oath was taken never to raise the incident. The boy's parents did not know how close their son came to a sorry end.

Norman loved his freedom (as his father) and could not let a glorious summer day go by (and school day) without feeling the sunshine on his back. He would take his handmade crab spear and troll the local rocks where some extremely large king crabs lived. He skipped between the rocks and bounced the spear interspersed with his gait to catch it; his hand and leg were not in synch and speared his fore leg with the barbs.

The local tram guard was a bystander and gathered

him up and headed toward the tram bound for the Prince Henry Hospital. The good Samaritan was holding Norman, but the spear had somehow fallen from his grasp and tore the flesh even deeper. Perhaps that was not as excruciating as a two year old who careered his dinky off the front balcony of their home about 15 feet or so and landed the handle bars embedded into his abdomen.

Or perhaps as a six year old pulling on a cauldron of hot oil in readiness for frying the catch of the day. Ursula had wrapped him in Bates Asalve and clean sheets. She was to visit him in the hospital over many weeks and during the road to recovery, they were to trial a new mercolised wax treatment for burns. It reburnt the skin and extended his recovery time. The doctors said that he would have been severely scarred if it had not been for the application of the Salve. Ursula said that it was either an arse or an elbow with Norman.

Living on the water bought about good and worse times. The boats were anchored in the bay in view of the house and we could see William's departure and arrivals from the front porch.

In later years, William and Norman were working together alongside the pier at La Perouse in readiness for heading out through the heads of Botany Bay for their next fishing expedition. William in the wheel house churning the engine and Norman assisting to lift the anchor for departure. Norman was winding the stern ropes until he yelled for his father to stop the engines. Below were two small figures lying motionless on the ocean floor. They winched the trawling net down and drew them from the bottom.

It seems the two boys had been watching the boat from the wharf and had become mesmerised with the eddy of the water from the engine. They were too close to the action and were sucked down to the sea bottom. It had only been minutes prior to the incident, as both gurgled and spluttered as they lay on the deck. They recovered and refused to give their names. A lucky escape for them and their unbeknown parents. They ran home.

A large part of our family history must also make mention that we have been blessed with some amazing and loyal companions. I give thanks and remembrance for Laddie, the long-haired Daschund; Simon and

Robbie, Tiger, Ginger, Pal and Peter who died on my birthday after 16 years of comradery and walking the rocks and beach with us. Father's most trusted of 17 years Ben; Benji the Shih-Tzu and Bobbie the big fat Retriever (who deserves a medal for pulling my daughter to safety from the bottom of our swimming pool!) Just thankful that we all have great lung capacity being swimmers!

Grandfather William and Norman

Norman was definitely a throwback from the Hobson family and had salt water in his veins. With all of his gusto, as a young man he joined forces with his father to build craft on the vacant allotment they had purchased alongside the family home. The romance of timber (plank) boats is still very much appealing to many but the man hours were intense and sometimes took up to two years and more to complete a 100-foot vessel. Sometimes they would enlist the help of an Italian by the name of Gigi who joined them and delighted them in preparing his signature dish on board, of fish soup with aromatic tomatoes and crunched handfuls of pasta and herbs. My father was still extolling the flavours all those years later.

Obviously there was always ample seafood to be shared at home from a good harvest, and it continued to provide well for the seafood shops and those locals who would look forward to buying straight from the beach on the trawler's return. Fish was always available at breakfast in Ursula's home, and Norman would relish several fried bream with Worcestershire Sauce on his return from an early morning sculling training at Leichhardt, Haberfield or Drummoyne. As any serious musician knows, any large boat deck holding ropes, tackle and nets is not complete without a piano on board. Yes, Bill serenaded most of Sydney sea life. He would drop anchor and sometimes play for an hour. How inspirational. The dolphins particularly responded by swimming both sides of the boat long after the music had stopped. How he loved nature. One of his favourites to play was Silent Night.

One occasion a startling event occurred. A massive whale must have been following in the wake of the trawler way off shore in cold deep waters. The whale rose on the starboard side without warning. He was longer than their boat. Both men were level when the whale breached the water and with a huge eye spied the two. The boat seemed totally dwarfed. So close was the whale it was thickly encrusted in barnacles, algae, weed and crustaceans. A paralysing thick mucus was showered over them, the bow and the deck. The whale stayed with them for some time and they were so alarmed that this monster could have so easily rolled their vessel.

The whale sounded and its giant tail, so powerful, crashed through into the depths and jarred and scuffed the boat as it did so. Their clothes were saturated with residue and no amount of washing would remove the stench. Eventually their garments were burnt as the odour was permanently imbedded in the fibres. It just dawned on me perhaps his lucky jacket was also burnt…Could this have sadly changed his mojo?

The weather was not always conducive so they would head for sheltered waters, but rain, hail or shine there was work to be done and fish to be caught in season. Having come from a sea-faring family we checked the barometer at home more than the clock as an indicator of the rise and fall of the weather and way below 'low' was a "no go". This did not say that freak storms did not occur.

Father spoke of THE freak storm. He was a young man and the boat was floundering through huge waves with his father at the helm. They were both running the gauntlet. Torrential rain and lightning was a bad mix. Water was crashing over the wheelhouse and the skies were thunderous. The big diesel heart kept grinding away and they prayed it did not stop as they would surely capsize.

William was not concerned that his vessel was anything but seaworthy but for his son who was fit, a light frame he did share concern. He would be washed overboard. William strapped him to the mast. A captain's call was not to be countermanded, so for hours Norman was frozen in time, literally. How frightening and how exact was Bill's decision. Both lived to tell the tale.

Many objects are salvaged at sea; dredged up with the day's catch and nets. Items from the cargo of the ship SS Emden as well some most unusual sightings in the calm of cold deep waters. Having been on one of their longer journeys they were to spot a Navy carrier motionless on the horizon. As they drew closer it revealed its cargo of huge wooden crates which were being hauled overboard. As the boat came within range, the crates contained brand new war planes as depicted by the drawings on the side.

William seemed to think that the long range orders for planes destined to assist the war effort were surplus after Armistice was declared. Obviously covered by insurance – they now lay in Davey Jones' Locker. Those two men certainly shared some wonderful times together.

When you are a daughter of a Seaman – Adventures Abound

The Southerly Buster's (cold southerly winds) were well known and experienced far too often in Botany Bay. One such storm or should I say cyclonic event in the 1960's is the stand out.

Having a re-direction, father's business was now focusing on developing pleasure craft, water skis and accessories. This meant that some of the products required continual testing. Towra lay in Botany Bay, now a heritage listed island and covered under Trust. It is a small, sheltered and protected island that has good beach access for boating. It lies across the bay and opposite the suburb of Sans Souci and Woolooware and beside Kurnell. It became a picnic destination and the chosen location for us to learn to water ski. I was in the early years of primary school.

I am unsure where the old-style Titanic life preservers came from (probably the authentic Titanic itself!) but they were more of a hindrance than a help and used to be placed over my head and tied beneath the armpit. The bulbous mounds of preserved material may have contained sawdust or some glutinous material as each fall to the water would render an upper cut to the chin and cause severe chaffing to the underarms.

To anyone who knows the mixed treachery of Botany Bay, it is not devoid of sharks. In hindsight I wonder if father ever considered it dangerous, because as a child I implicitly trusted him. As my skinny legs dangled beneath the water in less than calm seas in the middle of the bay, it would seem to a white pointer shark, as a prawn on a skewer. This in itself was incentive to master the art of skiing.

It was decided that Norman spent far too much time in developing his trade and we would invite his mother Elsie Ursula and brother Jack to enjoy a picnic on Towra. Mindful that Ursula was not the greatest water-lover but she may have enjoyed the leisurely speedboat ride across the bay. The day was hot and the breeze pleasant as we motored toward our destination. As a good shipwright, Norman was religious in distributing the seating weight in the boat with the heavier in the bow and the lighter toward the stern. He said the boat would ride better. The picnic baskets, swimmers and towels were stored forehead.

Elsie Ursula had been dubious about the outing to a remote island. Those days' women wore more demure attire and definitely no slacks. She appeared in her floral silk dress belted neatly at the waist and those reliable black practical lace up shoes selected for the day's outing. Jack was a single man and always quite dapper. His choice of attire obviously had been given more thought. He would have looked more at home on a jungle safari wearing beige light weight slacks, a green safari jacket with epaulettes open at the neck and a light coloured pith helmet to cover the sun and his usual tortoise shell framed sunglasses. Singing along the way to 'Summer Holiday' and Petula Clarke's 'Downtown' it was a very exciting and fun morning and we looked forward to our prepared picnic lunch and a swim; as for now our hair was being tousled by the warm breeze. All was right with the world and we had gran with us. Norman held the bow as all disembarked from our well-crafted plank vessel. The white sand was bliss and the water lapped as melodiously as an idyllic Pacific Ocean was expected. Our site was selected with some shade and all rugs were placed around the camp with the picnic centred. The coloured plastic plates and utensils gave a festive feel.

We all took a walk, meandering through the foliage toward the rear of the island and Norman gave commentary on various aspects of the island history and we were delighted to have stumbled across fresh oysters. A welcome luncheon entrée for the adults. All was going well on our picnic. The basketball was thrown around and luncheon began. Between the roast chicken, coleslaw and mother's best recipe of chocolate cake with rum icing, all hell broke loose.

My father surveyed the skyline and did not like what he saw. Black clouds appeared like a wall of soot and the smell of musty rain was in the air. It was raining well out to sea as sheets of rain blackened the skyline and jagged white clouds fell in shards. He instructed us to throw all the food and plates into the blanket as quickly as possible. We had little time before the eye of the storm hit, but we still had at least half hour to head home across the bay. We had life jackets (yeah right!) and paddles and spray jackets.

Within minutes, the rain began as droplets which poured down big and cold. The rain intensified and the hail hurt our arms and legs. The boat was cabinless so we had to endure all that the heavens were to throw at us. The rain was blinding and the waves had grown at least three times the height of our vessel. It was a southerly buster alright! The waves were crashing fast and furious – up and down as on a roller coaster and there was little visibility which tested the boat severely. The outboard motor was trying to perform miracles as the propeller was more out of the water than in. We were making no headway.

Ursula was petrified and Jack advised that he was concerned in case she suffered a heart attack.

Norman decided to change direction and head for the lee of Sans Souci shores. The bailer became our best friend as the waves broke relentlessly upon us. Although there was now so much water filling the boat that it was beginning to render the bailer almost useless. The big fellow upstairs was testing us and in one foul swoop all could change.

We were now saturated and bone-shaking with cold. Norman navigated toward Sans Souci and the waves were now breaking over the stern... not a good thing. As we came closer to shore, scant figures could be seen through the rain. They emerged from their cars no doubt also caught out from picnics.

They could see our dilemma and they came forward to assist. We needed to keep the boat's bow seaward otherwise on the side we could have rolled. Ursula was slumped beside Jack, eyes closed prepared for the worst. Rescuers pushed through the spume and held the boat stable, lifting her small frame to safety along with Jack. Ursula was yelling that we would all be killed and to leave my mother June and I at Sans Souci.

I was fine and was loving the excitement and had not given thought to any of us having been knocked unconscious. There was no boat ramp close by. Both Ursula and Jack no doubt thankful to be alive and on terra firma. Ursula's silk dress had shrunk revealing her very pale legs; her large straw hat fell lifeless on both sides. Jack in his pith helmet and distressed Gran leaning against each other both sipping brandy from a flask (used purely for medicinal purposes!). It came to me years later that three generations could have been lost that day.

The storm of all storms for our Peninsula

It was a very memorable May 1974. It was my able seaman father who read weather better than the Meteorologists. Father sounded the alarm once again to herald bad weather This would be the worst storm. He was correct it was not a storm; it was more like a cyclone. The area was not prone to cyclonic weather. The worst previous weather had come from the east or the south. This storm would come from everywhere.

Our home was brick but substantially we took advantage of the sea view from a floor of glass windows. They were not double glazed in those days.

There had been weather warnings to prepare for bad weather over Sydney.

Norman was the resourceful 'prepared tradie type'. Firstly the dogs were brought inside. He had seen bad weather with his father... worse on the ocean. That unpredictable part of nature. He looked worried all that day and was collecting towels and battening anything he could find down with nails. Father likened this storm to one previously met in the Nella Tub when crossing the tempestuous Tasman Sea on-route to New Zealand.

The captain was at the helm. We were quietly excited I guess you could say but the dogs told another story. They were slinking around and not making a sound.

There was no sleep to be had... we stayed awake all night. The wind and the rain joined forces... the rain deafening like hammers and the wind howling against the windows. The orders came to drag ballast from our rooms to hold fast against the windows which were being bent with the gale. These could break at any time. "More weight girls"! (Unknowingly for father we spent an inordinate time and money getting rid of the weight!). Now we were scared.

For hours the storm persisted and for hours we stood with our arms spread eagle around our mattresses with our body weights against the windows and the storm. Our arms were leaden and aching; our legs buckling with fatigue. The deeper night made it even more frightening as we could hear but not see tin tearing from the roofs, things flying and landing against the garage beneath, and items scraping against the brickwork… perhaps our neighbour June's outdoor setting was even flaying and tangoing through the air.

In the distance a cacophony of metal, collapsing bricks, timbers smashing, we were hoping all the time that our neighbours were safe but we needed to remain safely behind locked doors. Our windows were not water-tight. There was leakage a plenty… rivulets running across the timber floors from the lounge room into the kitchen.

This was not good. Excitement was now terror… perhaps our home would be demolished? We took short shifts when one could no longer hold the mattress. Our clothing was clinging to our bodies. The wind and rain was being swept around the window jambs. The cheap window latches were half opening and banging as that cyclone became bored and toyed with the idea of lifting the suckers out!

Well into the early hours of the morning there was silence. Unlike the urgency to open your Santa stocking as a young child, there was reluctance – it was like slow motion…what devastation was out there? Our legs were dragging, bodies heavy with sleep and aching limbs.

That cyclone had media coverage for quite some time. We fared better than some. Mother's dear friends June and Maurie and her mother and father Mr and Mrs Townsend were the original owners of the beautiful and iconic seafood restaurant 'The Paragon' perched on the rocks high above the ocean at the south end of Frenchman's Bay. It was so popular and the cuisine was excellent. Overseas travellers loved to eat there.

It was now badly listing. The cyclone had lifted the substantial timber footing and structure from the rocks where it had stood for 100 or more years and it was sliding into the ocean. There was debris everywhere. A family's livelihood vanished in the blink of an eye.

It has been explained to me from their family recently, that it took the family five years for the insurance claim to be investigated. It was heralded by a well-known judge who ruled that it was an Act of God and the best and most historic restaurant in La Perouse, sadly was never rebuilt. Particularly with the added weight of an environmentalist who pronounced that the site should be kept as "open space" in a national park? Plenty of open space. In fact, I do believe I had seen this same gentlemen enjoying meals at the Paragon.

As we walked further, we were also in awe that for many years a large dilapidated iron tanker had laid dormant on some old rusting slips not far from the restaurant. It was sizeable and weighed tons. It had been scooped up like a piece of greased-proof-paper from a child's lunchbox blowing across the playground. There she was thrown twisted into the sea a few hundred metres or so.

Botany Bay can be treacherous if you do not treat her with respect.

Unlike other storms, my father recited a sad story perhaps the likes of the tragic sequel of which the family were never aware. In those early days, there was not the sophistication of the Coroner that there is today...the forensic science which can now minutely detect DNA, genes, diseases and the like. William and Norman were trawling in Botany Bay and came upon the remains of a torso.

The bones were small as that of a young teenager. I am unsure whether the authorities were alerted... There had been an incident in the Bay many months prior. Two brothers had been sailing in a small jabot in Botany Bay and had not returned. The rumours were that two brothers had taken a boat sailing without the permission of their parents. They were also supposedly unable to swim. The ocean holds many a secret.

Troubled Waters Again – Farewell William Farrell

The party dress spun prettily as a 3 year old sang a ditty from her very limited repertoire and danced happily for her grandfather William. Joined by the family of choralists and supported by my father Norman, William arose from his bed as if on a rocking horse. I recall well the striped brown flannelette pyjamas which motioned toward me and William held my face in his hands with firmness and a little grin.

Unwittingly, this would be the last time I would sing for him.

Grandpa was normally not to be seen in the house;

sleeping on board boat; hauling net loads of unsuspecting fish into the hold of Nella.

William was not in any way house-proud or interested in domestics. This was where my father would also have received the same gene! It was all business. It was also according to my father that his father Bill spent no leisure time with his family or his sons. Norman said that his father saw him win only one of his many sculling races in 16 years and one day in Leichhardt he appeared and carried his sculls back to the shed. This was his way of showing his son he was proud without actually saying the words. They (of that era) were a stubborn lot but it would have meant the world to my father had William expressed his love and care openly. When Norman was working on the boats there was comradery but it turns out that William was very happy that my father's efforts on the trawlers had been gratis all those years.

In the late 1940's, Norman built a passenger craft M.V. 'Miss Flash' and registered the services of conveying tourists and small groups across the bay between La Perouse and Kurnell. The 'Occupation Health and Safety' Laws were not in force unfortunately, as one of the Professors from a university group was identified as using the cap of the spare fuel barrel to ash his cigarette which was located aft of the vessel. A lucky escape for all. He was sworn to and refused any further access to the launch service.

My father at 37 announced to his family that he and June Evans were engaged. My mother was very attractive with titian hair and a wonderful figure. She loved the beach and swam and bathed in the sun as often as possible. Her skin was very olive and she was always tanned and healthy. Along with her close friend June Hume, they would spend many hours on our local beach enjoying the sunshine and playing with their new babies and toddlers.

In her early years prior to marriage, mother was a seamstress and enjoyed working with David Nathan, (Trent Nathan's father) sewing in a workshop in Paddington NSW. She was totally at home modelling beautiful garments for overseas buyers which also included collections of swimsuits.

My mother, June apparently was a standout at the beach one day in a white one piece swimsuit which was bordered with black and white star trim on the v-neckline and legs. She would have me swimming as often as possible and after school was no exception. Even later when she became a nursing aide at the Prince Henry Hospital on the night shift, she needed little sleep and we would rejoice after school in the little white capped waves as she shoved me onto the next set of waves on my surfboard.

William had not been overjoyed at his son Norman's impending marriage particularly as his only working son at that time could not continue working on the boats. Norman now needed to help support his initiatives and future family plan. He sought engineering work away from the home environment at ICIANZ or now Orica.

My grandfather should not have been initially upset with my father's announcement as he and my mother had a long five year engagement!

Mother was inspiring. June was a free spirit; had boundless energy and was always happy and sang opera when she was polishing the floors and doing the domestics. I think you would also say she was good company. She was sporty and was a wonderful sprinter. She always shuddered that in her early teenage years she had been chased by a boy brandishing a knife down her local street and only that she had outrun him things had not looked good. Startlingly that boy later I was to learn was her brother Darcy. Darcy was later a long serving solider in the army and a Vietnam expatriate. He was a wonderful man but the two teenagers had been jumping on the bed in trampoline mode when the base broke and Darcy's nose was broken and bloodied.

He had a gross temper and grabbed a towel to his face and a large bread knife and chased his sister down Lord Street Newtown and across Unwin's Bridge Road Sydney. He certainly must have made a good soldier.

Mother loved to share luncheon and champagne with her good friends June Hume, Mary McCallum and some of her work colleagues to celebrate the Melbourne Cup. Bart Cummings, the world renowned horse trainer was her favourite sports person and was delighted when she had opportunity to meet him on one race day prior to her passing. She also loved her home and spent hours making everything shine. She loved summer.

Norman and June were married at Newtown and

you would not guess, it was raining, and mother's car broke down requiring her to walk the remainder of the way to the church beneath an umbrella. Not even that fazed her. Mother loved life and she was carefree. Her comments were that only death was the one thing you could not change.

One late afternoon on a hot sweltering summer day, mother raced to the beach for a quick swim prior to concentrating on the evening meal. In her usual exuberant style, she would rebound or leap from the shore up into the waves and she looked down between her arms when she caught a glimpse of a large shark propelling through the very wave she was headed. She hit that water with great trepidation and could do no more than swim faster than she ever had to shore. Forever she had asserted that no longer would the family swim at that time in the afternoon. She forbade us, as she thought it may have been feeding time for them. Good one mother!

Mother was such a kind and generous person and never begrudged helping grandmother Ursula or anyone with their chores. A basket load or two of ironing would always find its way into our house and be returned the next morning. My mother loved her grandchildren and accompanied them to the beach on school holidays just as she had done me.

William no longer had reliance on his son during those trawling expeditions and I am unsure whether Gigi was still his offsider on board. (I had seen William confined to bed during that little singing performance but I cannot confirm whether he had slight heart problems then which precipitated his accident). Either way, he was seen climbing the hill for the family home after he had thrown anchor in the bay and somehow found his way to shore. Blood streamed from his temples onto his jacket and shirt as several bystanders aided him.

Ursula phoned for assistance and he was admitted to hospital. He was not in a coma but very disoriented but was able to explain that the block and tackle on board boat had swung round and hit him in the head. Apparently, he lay on deck for hours and was lucky to regain consciousness and particularly to remember how to navigate back to the bay.

Perhaps his lucky seagull had divinely guided him to safety or perhaps his dear dolphins lead the way.

It seems a miracle that he was not hit overboard in which case his death may have remained a mystery (another one!)

William remained in hospital several days. Ursula received a phone call which gave the news that William had passed away. William had sustained one heart attack after another and had no chance of survival. He was 73. Again Ursula had taken a broadside losing yet another loved one.

Coogee Aquarium Baths, Proprietor William Farrell Hobson, my grandfather.

The Shark Arm Murder Mystery

The Shark Arm Murder of course needs a mention. The Hobson family seem always to be surrounded with intrigue…well why not a murder? (Gives a certain spice to the book, and as well it is our history).

The story and murder was always kept immortalised and was a favourite topic at our family gatherings.

Whilst the Hobson brothers (my father's uncles)

Charlie, Albert and William all had their differences, it was expected that they all pull their weight in running the family owned Coogee Aquarium, corner of Dolphin and Mount Street, Coogee NSW Australia (swimming baths).

April 1935, it was my grandfather William and brother Charlie who were fishing off the Sydney Heads. They were to haul a very large and weighty tiger shark into their nets along with the catches of the day. The brothers were always business men and opportunists. This shark would make them money!

The late 1800's and early 1900's was a time when public entertainment containing smoke, mirrors, shock, horror or magic was a certain bestseller. Such as the great escape artist Houdini who thrilled crowds with his performances.

Another certain winner was animals and how about mammals? The family archives produced an ageing document which was a Proposal and a Memorandum of Articles of Association to float a company by shareholding. The pages set out an extravagant venture to procure exotic animals from around the world and exhibit them at the premises of Coogee. This did not occur; perhaps the war had been a game changer. But it did not change the brothers' instinct for business.

The swimming season was ending and the shark would make a sensational attraction to the baths.

There would be a charge for admission at the turnstiles and the baths took on a theme park atmosphere. I can just imagine they would have devised the forward marketing plan to increase the sales of their popular Cadbury chocolates. Those winter stalwarts (the salt water baths were not heated) who came to swim must have burnt their heels skidding to a halt prior to taking that almighty leap off the diving board when that shark cast its gigantic shadow on the sides of the pool. Word spread throughout neighbourhood and the whole of Sydney came to ogle the captive monster.

The shark was at first listless and then became frenzied thrashing about until it regurgitated muck and fish carcasses into the pool. The most unexpected from this incident was the gruesome sight of a severed arm tattooed with two duelling boxers. The detectives were soon on the scene and our baths were closed for some time during the investigation.

Detectives interviewed persons of interest including

James Smith who had been following the papers on the shark arm case and identified the tattoo as being from his brother Edward who was found to have a police record.

Many leads were followed up and at some stage there was even an expectation that the murder was related to a crime syndicate. Wow! In the tiny little suburb of Coogee.

A crucial part of this story is that the shark had not bitten the arm but it had been sawn. The Shark Arm Case was closed but never resulted in a conviction.

The Court ruled that without a torso related to the severed arm there was no conclusive proof that the murder had taken place. Surely a technicality but the crucial piece of evidence did not exist.

The only ones to benefit from the whole case were, yes my great uncles who sold reams of admission tickets to the baths and of course many boxes of chocolates!

The Royal Truth Finally Uncovered

You have now read the previous chapters. But you still do not know the full story.

Neither did I. Until yesterday the 3rd June 2017.

My wonderful daughter phoned me late afternoon having discovered a recording which she located on the YouTube site with further pertinent information on Queen Victoria.

Tony Rennell's recording is entitled 'The Secret Q.V. Took to Her Grave'. Tony Rennell has an associated family member who was Queen Victoria's Physician.

The recording states that Dr. Reid was not only

Victoria's doctor but also a close confidante. It states that Dr Reid was made Victoria's Executor over her Last Will and Testament. Included in this will was instruction for Victoria's burial. There is also testament that her wedding ring (given by Consort Prince Albert) be placed on her left hand, and on her right hand, John Brown's mother's wedding band.

The recording confirms that Victoria had 9 children by the approximate age of 47 and she was adamant to increase her family. Based on concern for his Queen's health Dr. Reid strongly dissuaded Victoria from increasing her family. Mr. Rennell also openly states that it could not be discounted that she may have given birth to several more children.

Thank you Tony Rennell for your honest and inspiring account and for also posting your recording for all to share.

During the same conversation with my daughter I had also been trawling through photographs on the internet of the Royal Archives. It is a day I will never forget.

I do believe it changed my perspective in this Royal mystery. My heart sings a million tunes of love and thanks. My daughter provided me time in locating a rare photograph.

Here in front of me... rubbing my eyes...is a very tall, proud well-balanced John Brown. A somewhat mature and older John Brown unlike the usual popular "commercial photographs" of him pulling the pony trap with Victoria or esconced on the Balmoral Castle stairs with the royal canines.

My mouth agape. It is astonishing after all these years. I recognise this large kilted and heavily grey bearded gentleman! To my amazement, it is the man in the only photograph we had holding my father in his arms as a tiny baby in the rear of their home 'Rose Cottage' Randwick NSW Australia.

I am confident that gentleman holding my father is John Brown.

My assumption now is that John Brown is Elias Raycroft. They are the same person and the Raycroft name was used for convenience and identification for further generations

This is a huge find. All the pieces fit. This new photograph changes everything. Could it be that "John

Brown's body is not a "mouldin' in the ground" as the song says, at Crathie Aberdeenshire alongside his family.

This revelation brings a different flavour to this Autobiography. It is a turnaround. So it seems that Annie Raycroft may also be a convenient name. My gut feeling now is that Annie is the Mistress of the Robes as per gran's statement, and Victoria's good friend and confidant. She would therefore be the Dowager Anne Murray born Anne Home Drummond (1814-1897), as I have researched, Duchess of Athol and Lady Glenlyon between (1839-1846). I hope somehow this will be confirmed. It makes sense who else would you rely on to forever look after your children? Your closest and trustworthy friend. Who would you choose if necessary? An interesting thought?

I now assume that my gran knew her father very well. The inconsistencies on some of the documents signed by John and Annie. One it is their place of birth as the Isle of Bute and then again County Cork Ireland.

John and Annie were definitely on a mission. Sent to Australia by Victoria under trust. I had always wondered why they needed to retreat so far from England. Now that reason is so glaringly obvious. Everyone knew John Brown. Therefore, he would live undetected in the far-off island in the middle of the Pacific. Particularly the then remote La Perouse where he spent the remainder of his life. The furthest country from the UK.

Can we surmise that John's apparent death may have been orchestrated? How else his absence be explained or justified and what of the Duchess Anne? How did she remove herself from England under a veil?

John Brown is said to have died in 1883 in England. As our family Bible seems to tell a story, the three children journeyed from England to Australia on 1 January 1884. I have not seen or heard any recording or facts surrounding John Brown's funeral and only photographs of his last resting place in Crathie. Forgive me as I have not had the pleasure of visiting Crathie but there seems no epitaph or headstone which says, "here lies John Brown'.

I have read that Victoria's Dr Reid had a vehement dislike for the Highland Ghillie. Perhaps he was eagerly willing to assist Brown to leave the country.

How divisive a plan? A super spy story. I had always questioned why a burly, tough, strong leathery Scotsman who survived the rigours of Highland winters and was athletic enough to counter several attempts on Queen Victoria's life supposedly died so young. The Highlanders are well known in history as steely fighters. John Brown certainly had the presence to live up to that reputation. As we know he lived a long life. Just like all of my family.

Living in the same family home all those years, my father Norman unfortunately passed never knowing Elias was really his grandfather John Brown.

It is now making sense why John and Duchess Anne are buried hidden with no headstone in a site overlooking one of Sydney's beautiful iconic landscapes.

This is the REAL Love Story. John Brown cried always that he could not return to England. He must have made agreement with Victoria to accompany and care take his beautiful children Elsie Ursula, William and Daphne into adulthood. He may have walked away from the love of his life. The Book of Common Prayer which John held to his bosom the remainder of his life construed as the moment of his departure from England. I surmise this is when they may have become wed.

The inscription 'This is the Book of Love and Beauty' on the first page.

It now makes good reason that John was practising writing his pseudo signatures ahead of his new life. He fervently re-wrote his new name Elias Raycroft over and over again within the front cover.

How soul destroying for my great grandparents not to be destined to die together. In 1901, one could only imagine the distress John felt losing his only Victoria across cold deep waters thousands of kilometres from his birthplace.

From the very first paragraph it was inconceivable that my story and research would play out as it has. I am compelled to tell the true and untold story of their lives and honour our family. I am also compelled to declare that my descendants, in their final resting place in Australia, is not the resting place of their hearts. They were obviously duty bound.

So far it has evaded me why the name Raycroft was used and where it originated. Why and how did the name ELIAS evolve? As we have raised, several of the females on Elsie Ursula's maternal side were christened names which are anagrams of Alexandrina.

My hunch – could this same pattern been applied to Elias? Perhaps am I reading too much into this mystery; but please we cannot discount the consideration of a message of SAIL E (England?) or I LIE? The roguish John Brown seemed a reluctant and immoveable force and being aware of his introspective character, he "was not going down without a fight". He would have the last say in his churlish surrender. Somehow, call it divine intervention, but 135 years later someone finally received that message. That is almost like finding a "message in a bottle". Some people are born with premonitions; some ignore them and some foster them. Perhaps that is part of the legacy John has left for his family. **"I get it John"!!**

To be candid, the royal tryst had left me with mixed emotion. That a callous and brutal set of circumstances had torn these children, my family and their minders from their rightful home.

It changes my complexion of both my great

grandmother and the Highland Ghillie. A man of courage, strength and unswerving devotion to the love of his life and the monarchy. Yes Queen Victoria and John both died with very big secrets on their lips. How disturbing for all the players.

A young Victoria took on the world. She was destined for great things. But it must have been difficult being sought at the best parties, banquets and ceremonies to be catapulted into "the business" and its sombre realism. I have great admiration for women who are proud, strong, dedicated and who have the grace and presence to hold their own counsel.

Victoria and her daughter Ursula were from the same ilk and both rallied to meet expectation. Ursula was age 12 when Anne died, leaving her to raise her brother and sister in a new homeland. Ironically she would also be caretaking John Brown until his death.

Both women experienced the grief of losing their husbands early. Both were morbidly lonely as I now see. In a room full of people, it is just that. No comfort. I wonder how many buckets of tears they both shed behind closed doors.

Coining a phrase, 'the apple does not fall far from the tree'. Both were realistic women. Frivolous they were not. Indeed they both enjoyed entertaining and intelligent company. They appreciated life.

Victoria found solace with John after her greatest love Albert passed. I have read her pleasure was being surrounded by nature and wildlife. How carefree and bracing was it in those cooler misty mornings to pony trek along the mountain ridge on the Estate of Balmoral winding high above the River Dee accompanied by John and her entourage where a sumptuous picnic had been prepared most comfortably. Therefore Victoria was just as happy without the 'pomp and ceremony'. Ursula shared her thoughts with me that you could be just as happy with the "right one living in a tent". That speaks to me that money was not everything to these women. Now all is said and done, how very similar and uncomplicated they were in their basic of tastes.

Epilogue

My understanding is that my Grandmother was cousin to Duchess Alice, Countess of Athlone 1883-1981 who married The Duke of Gloucester, Henry Montagu Douglas Scott 1900-1974.

It would not be out of the question to assume that both Duchess Alice and my Grandmother Ursula may have sought opportunity to spend time together.

Duchess Alice and her husband Henry, The Duke of Gloucester made several trips to Australia one in 1935 to commemorate 100 years of Melbourne and the second was to visit and become patron to the newly built Prince Henry Hospital only five minutes' drive from our home in La Perouse in the adjoining suburb of Little Bay.

Epilogue

Uncannily Ursula's daughter Ena (Roby) as I best understand, met her husband Thomas Roby, a lawyer also having a connection to the board of the Prince Henry Hospital.

In 1945-1947 The Duke accepted the role of Governor General of Australia. Assuming their wealth, status and respect I need to wonder what was the attraction to Australian shores? Perhaps family??!

Harold and Daphne lived very close to the Governor Generals residence in Kirribilli. A ferry ride away from their home in Cremorne.

We discussed previously that Daphne as a young woman had been billeted. Could it be that Daphne actually billeted and lived with the same related Douglass family? Was that Douglass line part of the Montagu Douglas Scott family?

Was Harold Page Douglass a member of this family and then became betrothed years later?

Daphne and Harold were married on 18 April 1914.

This may be conjecture but Harold's father Alfred John Douglass purports as a partner in ownership of the Geelong Advertiser newspaper, Victoria in the

1880's and had a residence on Eastern Beach. Is this also a link to their past?

Could we also assume that this association in the industry provided Elsie's brother William his lifetime profession as a typesetter for the Herald newspaper in Broadway New South Wales?

I have acquired Harold's birth certificate which states his birthdate of 7 July 1883. His father Alfred John Douglass and mother Susan Land of Birmingham England. It can also be seen that Harold also had a living brother.

Harold and Daphne's home in Cremorne was transferred by David Douglas to Harold Douglass on 13 April 1921.

Research revealed there being Major Sir David John Montagu Douglas Scott educated at Eton College Windsor Berkshire England.

There seems much coincidence surrounding our family lives. The last twist to the puzzle is that having received Daphne Victoria Raycroft Allen Douglass's (the youngest of the three children of Victoria and John Brown) death certificate dated 15 November 1932.

Epilogue

It shook me to the core. Daphne died at the age of 39 from the blood disease of Haemophilia. A recessive and deadly gene which Victoria carried forward to several of her children.

One of which was Prince Leopold who died from the same curse at the age of 30.

My father Norman in his mid-teens, was never more uncomfortable when sitting in his beloved car named Suzie in Oxford Street Sydney. Why uncomfortable?

Whilst father William was navigating the pacific coastline Elsie Ursula would coincide her visits to the city. On these shopping expeditions Norman was relied upon to accompany his mother to and from the city to assist loading the parcels.

She was the sole shopper. Strangely, they would arrive at closing time of Mark Foys around 5 pm. Hours later Elsie would return to the vehicle in darkness with Norman usually asleep.

How he must have begrudged this chore. My father mostly in his fifties did not leave home to shop for himself but organised a men's apparel traveller from David Jones to visit our home to select his clothing.

His mother must have certainly impacted his abhorrence of shopping.

Gran was devastated when her eldest son Norman had been conscripted to the Army for the imminent WWII.

The training and manoeuvres took place at Greta, Hunter Valley New South Wales. Norman was to be stationed for a twelve month period with some friends including his best friend, Flight Officer Matt Hickson.

As we know my father was fit and healthy and he, as all men, considered their duty and the safety of their country paramount.

After many months word arrived that my father had been discharged from his duties at Greta and that he would certainly not see overseas action.

Norman returned home confused and upset. How does something like this happen??

Norman forever carried with him ashamedness. Unable to meet his own expectations of support to the war effort. Many of his mates died and also his friend Matt Hickson tragically in a routine training flight.

Flying past in an air show in and around Windsor/Richmond air base he lost control of his plane and plummeted into a hill. My father was devastated.

Norman and his father, being shipwrights, were then commissioned to design a boat for reconnaissance missions channelling up through the reaches of Papua New Guinea.

The craft would have a shallow draft to navigate close to the coastline and included large portholes in the gunnels which housed machine guns. This boat was later impressed by the Government.

Thankfully this project stemmed Norman's grief at having been discharged involuntarily from the army. He finally felt pride in his valuable contribution.

www.ingramcontent.com/pod-product-compliance
Lightning Source LLC
Chambersburg PA
CBHW031421290426
44110CB00011B/473